Every Step of the Way:
How Four Mothers Coped with Child Loss

by
Anne Dionne
Deborah LeBouf Kulkkula
Yvonne Lancaster
Jane Maki

PublishAmerica
Baltimore

First printing

At the specific preference of the author, PublishAmerica allowed this work to remain exactly as the author intended, verbatim, without editorial input.

ISBN: 1-4241-3080-8
PUBLISHED BY PUBLISHAMERICA, LLLP
www.publishamerica.com
Baltimore

Printed in the United States of America

In remembering and celebrating the lives of our children, we dedicate our book to the families of sons and daughters who have gone before them. May they have the courage, faith and strength to know the meaning of Midrash Tov's words:

"Immediately before the rise of the morning star,
The night is at its darkest before the dawn..."

Acknowledgements

Our thanks to our families, friends and all those who have helped us along the way with our own personal grief journeys. Through their love and support we have survived to tell our stories. We hope to keep the memory of our children—Michael, Christopher, Peter John and Brian—in the hearts and minds of generations to come.

A special thanks to our in-house editor, Neil Ian MacKillop. His valuable working contribution and unwavering support has our gratitude and respect.

INTRODUCTION

Life is full of bittersweet moments...

The lack of visibility that windswept October night did not stop the determined women. They forged ahead, three in all, a fourth waiting—each on a private mission the other knew nothing about, each heading for the same destination, the Kulkklua home, a neat, New England homestead nestled on a narrow road, deep in the woods.

Two of the three women traveled together, talking softly, sharing the latest family news. During their conversation, Anne Dionne, a soft-spoken, pretty woman with large hazel-eyes, never took her attention away from the dark road ahead, while she listened and chatted with her long-time friend Jane Maki, a passionate, feisty woman who was a retired nurse. The weather on the October night was relentless and pounding against them as they traveled. Under normal circumstances, none of the women would have ever ventured out on such an inclement night. But each felt a powerful force moving them toward one another, in spite of the challenging weather.

On the other side of the city, Yvonne Lancaster had just arrived home from work, a precarious 90-minute drive, in the stormy night. She had seen Deb Kulkkula's invitation to join a writer's group to explore the possibility of writing a collective book about coping with grief, in a general context. Undaunted by her husband's concern to stay home, she too ventured back into the wind-swept night. Calling ahead, she let the Kulkkulas know she was on her way.

Meanwhile, Deb and Peter Kulkkula prepared for their guests. The house was warm, with the aroma of hot mulled cider and freshly made doughnuts. Peter set the table carefully with little snack plates for cheese, crackers and fresh fruit. Making their guests feel at home had always been an important part of the Kulkkula's family doctrine.

Yvonne had met the Kulkkulas nine years prior at a Compassion Friends meeting; a support group for bereaved parents. The Kulkkulas had just lost their young son, Peter John, 19, in a tragic accident involving car repairs in their very own backyard. The Kulkkulas, even though newly bereaved, reached out to help other parents who had lost their children. This was their immediate way of coping with their own fatal loss. Yvonne, having lost her own son, Brian Richard, 19, eight years prior, in a car accident caused by a drunk driver, was both surprised and amazed by the way the Kulkkulas were facing their sorrow.

As she observed the Kulkkulas reaching out to help others, and listening to the circumstances of their personal tragedy, she realized that this was something she would have found impossible to do early on during her own grief journey. It brought home the thought that there is no "right or wrong" way to grieve. People who experience loss often go through their own personal journey which has no time-frame, no map, and no formula for surviving the physical and emotional trauma that encompasses the magnitude of losing one's child.

The porch light beaming from Kulkkula's quaint New England home was a welcoming sight to Anne and Jane. Anne forewarned Deb, a woman with an enviable picture-perfect complexion and sparkling blue eyes, that she had a cold, and didn't want her or Peter to catch it. This did not matter to Deb, as she embraced her friends when they arrived with her well-known and much celebrated hug. Deb's famous and much coveted hugs have been shared with hundreds of bereaved people during their darkest days.

Peter, bearded and laid-back, reminding one of a college professor, and an all around good guy, greeted the women and left the room to tend to his elderly mother upstairs. It was easy to see that the Kulkkulas were good-hearted folk.

As Anne and Jane were shaking off the wetness of the night and getting settled in the cozy living room, the phone rang. "I can't find your house", said Yvonne frantically. "I can hardly see where I'm going. I think I should go back home…" "Yvonne, let me send Peter after you," Deb said. "Let me put him on the phone."

"Where are you calling from?" Peter asked. "I'm in front of the Laundromat on John Fitch Highway."

"I'll be there in 15 minutes," Peter said. "No, that's too much trouble, Peter," Yvonne insisted. "Not at all, I'll be right there. I have a green-colored van. I'll flash my lights so you'll know. You can either follow me, or we can leave your car where it is."

"I'll follow you," Yvonne said. "It will be easier later on."

While Peter left to rescue Yvonne, the other three women talked about their sons' deaths due to different sets of circumstances. Anne's son, Michael, 19, was killed in a car accident on a foggy night in May, only one house away from his own. Jane's son, Chris, 30, was robbed and murdered as he walked home from a restaurant after an evening with friends, and Deb's son was mortally injured while working on a car that collapsed and fell on top of him.

"I've been doing a lot of thinking about writing a book which deals with grief—more so in a general way—so it would capture all people who are struggling with loss," Deb said as she offered fresh chocolates to Anne and Jane. "I've been keeping a journal since Michael died, and I have found that it's therapeutic to be able to write down my thoughts and feelings as I try to deal with the magnitude of having lost my son Michael," Anne said, with moist hazel eyes looking from one woman to another. Like Jane, Anne is a registered nurse working in a local doctor's office. "I can honestly say," Anne added, "that I've made a commitment to try and deal with my grief in a healthy way. I want to help others who are going through this experience. I want to keep Michael's memory alive…" her voice trailed off.…

"Chris was a victim of violence. His life was cut down by thieves and murderers. His life counted for something wonderful and great and I want others to be influenced in a positive way. His life was an example of love, caring, and strong family ties. I know I'll never have him back, but it's a dream of mine to write about Chris—to tell others what happened to him, to our family. We'll never, ever be the same," Jane said with passion and conviction. "This is a spiritual, emotional and physical trauma that will remain with my family forever. I have been keeping what I call my 'Chris Journal.' It's a safe place for me to talk to my son."

As a teacher, writer, social activist and entrepreneur, Deb had many contacts and acquaintances throughout the New England area. Many people who had heard the tragic news about the loss of her son, Peter John, reached out to her—hence, she reached out to others early in her bereavement.

"You know," Deb said sitting crossed-legged on the pretty white brocade sofa surrounded by family photographs, "I feel so badly for all who grieve over the loss of their loved ones. So many people have reached out to me. I feel their anguish, too; and it's difficult to separate them out from parents who have lost children…"

Peter finally reached Yvonne. She saw the lone dark van with lights flashing through the downpour. She immediately flashed her lights as well, signaling where she was. Both Peter and Yvonne left their vehicles to greet one another. Peter yelled through the rain. "Do you want to follow me, or would you rather leave your car here?" "I'll follow you, Peter. As long as I can see your tail lights, I'll be okay. Just go slowly," Yvonne said grasping the clasp of her hood with both hands. With water speckled glasses, Peter gave a quick nod yes and jumped back into his van, leading the way.

Yvonne followed Peter closely, wondering if she had lost her mind. Somehow, she felt a strange sense of urgency to meet these women, and decided she would keep on going, no matter what. Oddly, the foggy windshield that had been obscuring Yvonne's vision suddenly began to clear.

The house was barely visible through the sheets of rain. However, the small porch light appeared as a beacon of warmth and hope through it all. Peter led the way—both he and Yvonne shook off the rain in the library foyer like two pups. Deb, Anne and Jane left the living room to greet the wet travelers. Mission completed, Peter left the room, returning to the second floor. Ah, the luxury of Deb's hug! Yvonne thought it was nice to see her again after nine years. Even though Yvonne was meeting Jane and Anne for the first time, she felt her mother's heart and soul adhere to the other women. A mood of tenderness and compassion for one another permeated the room as they all sat down in the cozy kitchen for hot mulled cider and fresh doughnuts. Peter joined them, assisting Deb with the goodies.

As the women sipped the much-appreciated hot beverage, they found it difficult to choose between the choices of condiments to sprinkle on the warm doughnuts—powdered sugar? Cinnamon and sugar? Or nutmeg and sugar? They spoke in generalities about their lives, families and work life. Yvonne was a writer—having worked as a newspaper columnist for many years. She was currently a human resources professional in a large pharmaceutical company. Her life-long passion for writing never stopped, but was one of the mainstays in her life. Jane, having retired as a nurse, was now an integral part of a family seasonal camping business in New Hampshire. Deb was focusing a great deal of time producing programs for the local cable network. Peter was part of this effort as well. As mentioned earlier, Anne, a nurse, worked in a local doctor's office. She gave enthusiastic kudos to her employer for his effort in being so understanding and compassionate since the death of her son. Through Anne's gratitude, her employer was presented with the "Compassionate Employer Recognition Award" through The Compassionate Friends organization.

Since Yvonne was late in arriving, Deb explained how the women had discussed the possibility of coming together with a book project surrounding grief. "I think my aim as a bereaved parent is to share my experience with others in order to show that grief surrounding the loss of one's child is the greatest grief one can experience, and survive," Yvonne said in her soft, husky voice. "I've always worried that my son would be forgotten after I'm gone. This would be a way to celebrate his life too. I must admit, that it is taking a great deal of courage for me to do this. If we band together, I think it would give me the internal fortitude I need."

As the women talked, they realized they shared many things in common. They all lost sons, 3 of them at age 19. They all lived within 10 square miles of one another, and all had surviving children. Two had lost their only sons. Three had lost their sons to accidents. All had been independently writing about their experiences as a bereaved parent. They all wanted to express themselves in a way that would help other bereaved parents. Two were nurses, and two were writers. Three of the women were associated with The Compassionate Friends.

Deb, Anne, Jane and Yvonne came to understand that rainy, windswept night in October 2002, they indeed had come together through fate perhaps; nonetheless, they were connected in life and death with each of their sons, Peter John, Michael, Christopher and Brian. They came to realize that through their pain, suffering and fortitude they were truly all on a mission of love to help others, and to write about the sons they had lost.

The rain battering the kitchen window ceased. It was quiet as the women each gathered their thoughts along with cups and plates, bringing them to the sink. "Where do we go from here?" Deb asked as she covered the remaining goodies. "Focus, I think we need focus and direction," Jane said. "What if we met once a month—it doesn't matter where," Jane said, "as long as we meet and figure out our project together." All agreed. "My husband Neil is a writer and editor. I'd like to offer his experience to help organize us, and assist us with compiling our work. He can keep us on track. He's used to deadlines." Yvonne said. "He'll do anything I ask of him," she adding laughing.

It was agreed. The four women would meet once a month at Yvonne's house, since she commuted long distances to work everyday. It was a way to help her with her time, and include her ailing husband who was a kidney patient.

So the seeds of the project were planted, complete with a mission and a goal. They supported one another through the coming year with encouragement, round robin sessions, and an unyielding commitment to help others in their grief journey through life.

As Jane, Anne and Yvonne left Deb and Peter's home, the smell of damp leaves and clear skies greeted them.

The moon, visible now, added light and hope to their mission of love and compassion...

PART I

Anne's Story
Michael Steven Dionne
March 30, 1982 - May 15, 2001
Three Years Later

CHAPTER 1

A moment frozen in time

On May 15, 2001, my husband, Steve, and I set out for a trip to Baltimore in my father-in-law's Winnebago. My parents came with us. Our daughter, Kelly, was scheduled to graduate from college there on May 21, and we left early to give ourselves time to tour the Washington, DC, area.

Our 19-year-old son, Michael, decided to stay behind and help my father-in-law with the family business where he worked as an automobile mechanic. Michael had a plane reservation and was scheduled to meet us in Baltimore on May 20 so that he could also attend his sister's graduation. My husband and I kissed Michael goodbye early that morning, then we started out on the nine-hour drive. We had dinner at the campground when we arrived and went out to do a little shopping. We went to bed just before midnight. Not much time passed when I was awakened by a soft knock.

"Did you just hear a knock on the door?" I asked Steve.

I listened for a few seconds and decided the noise must have come from twigs blown by the wind. But less than a minute later the knock was much louder and more urgent.

We jumped out of bed and went to the door. Two police officers in uniform and a member of the clergy were standing outside. One of the officers asked us to step outside; he said they needed to speak to us. Steve went outside while I rummaged through the closet for something to put on over my nightclothes.

I was sure my heart would either explode or jump out of my body. I remember praying aloud repeatedly as I fumbled with my jacket,

"Please God, don't let it be Michael!" Once I was outside the camper, one of the officers introduced the three visitors. Then he said, "Your son Michael was involved in a motor vehicle accident this evening." He hesitated a moment. I heard him say, "It was fatal." Steve and I stood motionless. The officer repeated those awful words, "It was fatal."

From that moment on our lives were changed forever.

We stayed outside the camper with the police officers for a while. I wanted to know more details. We were told that there had been two fatalities.

So many thoughts were going through my mind. Whose car were they in? Who was the other person who had died? Where did the accident happen? I envisioned Michael in the back seat of a friend's car. It never occurred to me that Michael could have been the driver. The police didn't know who the other deceased person was, but they told us the accident took place at 43 Arbor St. in a van.

Then it all rushed in on me.

That meant Michael was probably the driver and that the accident occurred in front of our next-door-neighbor's house.

I was shocked, then horrified.

The officers offered telephone numbers and their support, then left.

We learned later that Michael and a few friends were at our home watching a baseball game when a friend called for a ride to join them. Michael had driven my van with another young man to pick up the friend who lived a little over a mile from our house. The weather was rainy and foggy. On the way back to the house, Michael lost control of the van coming around a bend, skidded and hit a tree in our next-door-neighbor's front yard. The friend in the back seat died instantly. Michael had a weak pulse when the emergency personnel arrived. He was given CPR and transported to the hospital. He was pronounced dead at 10:52 p.m., forty-five minutes after the initial 911 call. The young man who rode in the front passenger seat survived with moderate injuries. None of the boys had worn seatbelts.

Neither Steve nor I outwardly expressed emotion while the officers had been there.

We went back inside the camper where we both collapsed on the bed and held each other. Steve wept uncontrollably, and all I could do was to say over and over again, "I'm so very sorry."

My tear ducts seemed frozen. I felt like I had received a severe blow which knocked the wind out of me, and I needed to get back up. I didn't understand at the time, but I realize now, that I was in a state of shock. I believe shock is nature's defense against the severest of emotional traumas.

My parents had been sleeping in the back bedroom of the camper. My 81-year-old father came to us and asked if something was wrong. I said, "Dad, Mike was in an accident. I'm very sorry, but we have to leave now." My father was visibly shaken.

I went back outside the camper with my cell phone and called the police department in our home town for more details. I was told that Michael's best friend, Brett, was the other person who had died. I was told that my father-in-law had been notified and he had gone to the hospital.

Then I called the hospital. The charge nurse told me Michael's body would be taken to a facility where the medical examiner would perform an autopsy. I realized we would not be given the opportunity to see Michael due to the distance we had to travel.

Part of me wanted to be with Michael; however, part of me felt thankful that I wouldn't see his lifeless body. I didn't know if I could handle that. Subsequently, I have regretted not being with him that night. My father-in-law had declined the opportunity to see Mike because he didn't want to remember him that way. I felt great sorrow that Mike was alone, without someone who loved him being there.

While I was still outside the camper I heard my mother wailing. I went inside. My mother said she believes in miracles and that she was going to pray for Michael's healing. I told her Mike was not going to be all right. She asked me if Mike died, and I told her he had. While she wept openly, I asked her to be strong for me. I was sorry I couldn't offer consolation.

I was desperately trying to keep myself from losing control. It was the most difficult struggle of my life.

Kelly, who had been staying on campus, arrived at the campground soon after the police officers left. She and her boyfriend had been driven by a school counselor.

I hugged her and said, "I'm so sorry, Kelly, but we have to go home." I was emotionally frozen. Kelly fought back tears as she told us about a message she had received to call Leominster Hospital. She knew that couldn't bring good news. She had hoped the message would be about an elderly family member, not her only sibling. The emergency room nurse informed her that Michael had been in an accident and that her parents were not aware of it. When Kelly asked if he was all right, the nurse replied, "No, he didn't make it. Can you notify your parents?" Kelly was badly shaken. She said, "I can't tell my parents that!" She asked the nurse to have local police notify us and gave the nurse the address of the campground.

Kelly said goodbye to her boyfriend, and then we prepared to leave for the long journey home.

I didn't realize my father still believed Michael was alive. My mother hadn't told him. He asked me if Mike was going to be okay. I told him that he would not. My father asked, "Are you saying that Mike died?" I told him the truth. My father was dazed, and then he cried. I asked him also to be strong for me. I was very worried that either of my parents would collapse before we had a chance to get home.

Leaving the campground was a challenge. Steve quickly disassembled lines and hoses from the camper site. We had towed a car down to Baltimore. The plan had been for Michael to drive the car back home after the trip. Several times while we were hooking the car up to the camper, Steve collapsed against the car in uncontrollable tears. He was inconsolable.

I became very concerned that Steve would not be able to drive us home. He was the only person who had the skills to drive the camper, and it seemed like there were no other choices. I begged Steve to sit for a while and rest prior to leaving. He said he couldn't rest and just wanted to leave. Steve was so distraught and cried intermittently throughout the trip home. How we ever got home safely is a mystery to me even to this day.

The ride home seemed like an eternity. Except for Steve, everyone seemed frozen. No one spoke. No one slept. No one cried openly. The radio was off. There was only silence. We traveled through the night and into the morning. The trip took nine hours.

During the ride home, I felt an urge to call the organ donor bank. This seemed strange because I had never given any thought to it before, and the family had never discussed it. At 5 a.m. Steve made a brief stop at a rest area. I went outside with Kelly and my cell phone. I hadn't told Steve my plan.

That was the moment when I finally cried. I told the person on the other end of the phone about our situation. Just hearing myself say "My son was killed in a car accident last night" produced uncontrollable sobbing. I choked out the words, "I want to donate whatever we can." While the person asked routine questions, I sent Kelly back to the camper to obtain Steve's verbal consent. I could see Steve through the camper window. I watched with great sadness as he buried his face in his hands and wept.

The week of Michael's death was a very busy time. Visitors came. There were deliveries of flowers and food. Out-of-town guests and family members arrived.

I felt as though we were rushed to make funeral and burial arrangements. As I look back on that week, I wonder how grieving parents can be expected to rush through such decisions as though they are casually planning a day trip. After all, Michael was our son; he was in our lives for 19 years. How could we make such important decisions in a few hours?

I believe my state of shock served me well during the early stages of grief. At Mike's funeral I was able to greet people with hugs and a smile. I did that without tranquilizers or other prescription drugs. Today, I can't recall most of the people who attended. I just remember having a strong desire for Michael to be proud of his mother. But I do remember Charlie, one of the first responders who treated Michael. He came to the funeral and sobbed as he said, "I told the crew we weren't giving up on this one."

I was able to function at a high enough level to make decisions, submit insurance claims, and write thank-you notes. The first few weeks felt surreal. It seemed that time stood still; life stood still. I wanted to throw away my watch because time no longer made sense to me.

I remember thinking that I was strong, that I could handle the situation well. I remember feeling surprised that I hadn't really cried all that much during the first three months. I wondered whether I was really that strong or if it was normal not to cry. It wasn't until about four months after Mike died that I started to cry a lot. I cried much more frequently during the second year, and still cry freely at times during my third year. I now believe I was in denial for many months.

I felt traumatized by Michael's death physically, emotionally, mentally, and spiritually.

On the fourth day after Mike died it occurred to me that I was forgetting to eat. It was difficult to sleep peacefully. Mike was on my mind all my waking hours, and I dreamed about my loss at night. I felt an awful emptiness that I can only describe as a hole in my soul.

We sold the camper two weeks after Mike died. I didn't think I could ever travel in it again. I threw away the nightclothes I had been wearing when we received notification of his death.

As the weeks and months progressed, my greatest challenge was missing my son and knowing that he wasn't coming back again. This realization brought an ocean of tears. Many things could trigger my tears, such as certain songs, sights, memories, thoughts, and comments from other people. I never knew what or when.

I felt as though I was living in the "Twilight Zone" in the beginning. It was difficult to concentrate or remember. I dreamed about cemeteries and loss almost nightly for many months.

During the first few months I visited the cemetery on a daily basis. I would sing to my son sometimes, songs I had sung to him when he was a very young child. I kept a fresh supply of flowers as well as photos, angels, and other symbols of loving remembrance at the gravesite. I would sometimes go to the cemetery more than once.

I had difficulty letting go. I sometimes had a desire to bring Michael home from the cemetery. I struggled with the concept of his body being buried in the ground where I couldn't see him anymore. I recall sometimes lying on the grass while I cried and talked to my son.

I sought ways to feel Michael's presence by doing things like kiss his photos as I walked past them. I felt obsessed with my loss. I looked for images of Michael wherever I went. I noticed young men in public places who resembled him in any way, and I would watch them for a while.

The reality of my loss was so hard to accept. Pretending I could change my circumstances was far less painful. I began to fantasize that I could see Michael again by using bargaining techniques; but, I always knew the difference between the fantasy and reality. Once I was standing on a bridge while watching boats and water skiers below. I thought that I would be willing to bungee jump off that bridge, fly up in a space shuttle, or even live in Bosnia, just to see Michael again for one minute.

CHAPTER 2

Feelings of guilt

I knew that losing a child is every parent's nightmare; however, I never really believed it would happen to us.

I was angry. Losing my child made no sense to me. I kept trying to figure out why this happened, but I couldn't. I was trying to find an answer for a question that was inexplicable. Even if someone could offer a reason, there would never be an acceptable one for me. I felt victimized by life and death. My son's death felt like the ultimate breach of fairness. After all, my husband and I are responsible people and have a good marriage. We have a nice home, and we provided ample love and support to our children.

Many people have said we were wonderful parents. How could this happen to us, and not to our friends and neighbors? I wondered why we were singled out. I began to believe that parenting has little to do with how your children's lives turn out, and that life is a crap-shoot.

My son had driven the vehicle in which he and his best friend were killed. At first I felt very angry with Michael, but I couldn't remain that way because I loved him so and mourned his loss. I didn't allow myself to feel angry with God because my faith was helping me to cope with my loss.

I felt bitter when parents spoke about how well their children were doing. It was difficult to listen to parents who complained about their children.

In my quest to find reasons, I was feeling a sense of guilt.

I couldn't help wondering if I had failed him somehow. I believed that I should have been able to protect him from harm. I was plagued with questions. How was I to blame for what happened? Was there something I could have done to prevent this outcome? Did I deserve this pain and suffering? Was I being punished for what I did or didn't do?

Each time I asked the questions, the answer was the same: My husband and I adored our son and did everything we could to keep him safe and give him a good life. If I couldn't blame my husband or myself, who then? Did this mean that Michael's death couldn't have been prevented? Michael had an excellent driving record. He did what millions of teenagers have; he drove too fast one night. The difference was that he died while the majority of teens have gotten away with it.

I found it difficult to cope.

Several times while in a restaurant, I excused myself from the table when I heard a baby crying. I found myself escaping to the ladies' room because I couldn't control my tears. I wasn't quite sure why crying infants triggered such a strong grief reaction.

I thought a lot about babies for quite some time. My mind went back to the time of Michael's birth, which seems like yesterday. At that time ultrasounds were not being performed on a routine basis, and we didn't know the sex of our child during the pregnancy. Somehow I knew in my heart that I was having a boy. I even promised my husband that I would be giving him a son. I recall rhythmically massaging my abdomen during each contraction while silently saying, "Michael, I love you very much." Were the tears I was shedding for crying infants in restaurants really for my own baby?

Months after Mike's death, I realized I needed to feel joy again. I had gone too long without it. It was difficult to be in social situations with friends who were having a good time. I wanted to be among friends, but I wasn't happy. I worried that my presence would make others feel depressed, so I laughed and did my best to contribute to the gaiety. I don't know when the joy returned; it was a very gradual process.

I survive one day at a time. Some days are easier than others.

These things have been the key to my survival: family, support systems, employment, and spirituality.

I feel that I am doing well with my grief. I have strong faith, and my spirituality has helped bring a measure of peace. I believe that grief offers choices. You can either die with your child, or you can honor his life and yours by choosing to live fully. I am not bitter. I see Michael's life as a beautiful gift which my family and I were given for 19 years. It's up to us to take that gift and allow it to continue to bless our lives by discovering what he had to teach us.

My husband, Steve, and I have been married for 28 years. We have one daughter who is living, and one son who died. We have always been a very close family. In some ways Michael's death has brought us closer. Although many parents have known the pain of losing a child, my spouse and I are the only two parents who share the bond of losing our son Michael. We share so many special memories of Michael.

Our family keeps Michael's memory alive, and that has been a very important part of our survival. We have occasion to be with Michael's friends at times. Being with them helps us to feel Michael's presence. We celebrate the date of Michael's birth. We remember him in a special way during the holiday seasons. Our family presents a scholarship award to a graduating senior annually at our local high school in Michael's memory.

Our daughter, Kelly, recently married Eric Arcacha, the wonderful young man who was with her on the night of Mike's accident, and who has supported her through the most difficult trial of losing her brother. They honored Michael's memory on their wedding day in thoughtful and sensitive ways.

Two of Mike's closest friends were ushers at the wedding; and together they accompanied me to my seat. The two young men carried Mike's photo and a candle to the front of the church in the procession.

At the reception site, a table was placed near the function room with a nice basket filled with blue spruce saplings attached to a lovely poem in Michael's memory. Next to the basket was an 8" x

10" photo of Kelly with her brother which was taken during a summer vacation at Lake Erie. While I had worried that my daughter's wedding might bring much sadness due to Mike's absence, it turned out to be a lovely and joyful event.

I believe the best chance for a healthy resolution of grief comes by allowing yourself to work through it, not by repressing or denying it. Grief therapy has helped me in that process. Through it, I've learned that a tear filled day is not a bad day, but rather a day when I'm allowing expression of my grief. I've also learned to be more open with my family concerning my grief and to encourage them to do the same. Many bereaved parents never see a therapist. It is my belief that people must handle grief in their own way.

Talking about grief, especially with other bereaved parents, has helped me cope with my loss. I joined with two other mothers and started a bereavement support group at my local church.

I would not wish this kind of grief on anyone; however, knowing I am not alone has brought comfort. It is not possible to know the pain of losing a child unless you have actually experienced it.

Some bereaved parents may seek professional help and use prescription drugs short-term; however, I believe bereaved parents are the experts, they are the most qualified to help other bereaved parents. The Compassionate Friends is an organization of bereaved parents who offer support to each other and who reach out to the newly bereaved. The organization also has a chat room on their website that offers support. I've met some wonderful people in the chat room who have suffered unfortunate tragedies, and we have been able to offer mutual support to each other. After several months of visiting the chat room, I was asked to become one of the weekly moderators, and that is going very well.

Returning to work has been therapeutic for me. I enjoy my work as a registered nurse in a busy family practice.

On my first day back to work three weeks after my son died, I felt as though I had stepped out of the "Twilight Zone" and into a more normal world. For the first few months it was very difficult not to think about my loss many times during the workday.

I took my son's photograph off my desk. It was too difficult to look at his picture while I was working. During that period of time I frequently cried in my car as I drove home. I was able to handle my thoughts and emotions better as the months progressed.

Now I find focusing on the concerns of other people takes my mind off myself. It is particularly rewarding when I can help to promote well being in someone else.

I've been fortunate to have the support I needed from my employer, David Spiegelman, M.D., who is a wonderful, compassionate man. My co-workers have also been kind and supportive. Last year I nominated my employer for The Compassionate Friends Employer Recognition Award. The award is given annually to employers who show special sensitivity and compassion to an employee who has suffered the loss of a child. The organization's Regional Coordinator presented the award to Dr. Spiegelman at our office.

I believe the support is so vital to people who are trying to reintegrate into the work force after suffering a devastating loss.

I believe regular exercise, a healthy diet, and adequate sleep are beneficial in coping with grief. Losing a child made me feel vulnerable and off balance.

If my physical health is compromised, my problems seem amplified. I felt fatigued for many months after losing Michael. When the depression set in, it didn't help matters. Taking better care of my physical health gives me more energy to face the day and promotes a healthier mental attitude.

Soon after my loss I decided I would do everything I could to work through my grief, especially during the first year. I had heard stories about people who never dealt with their grief, only to suffer physical and emotional problems years later. I wanted to give myself the best chance I could to heal from the severest injury of my life.

One of the greatest challenges during the first year was allowing each person in my family to cope in their own way.

I didn't want to celebrate Christmas in the traditional way; however, our daughter needed to have a normal Christmas. We had to compromise on things such as the tree and gifts. I couldn't bear to put up our traditional tree, so we bought a small artificial tree with fiber optic lights. Instead of buying a lot of gifts for our family, we adopted a needy family and bought gifts and dinner for them in memory of Michael.

I needed to feel Michael's presence on the holidays, so I lit candles beside his photo. I kept a candle lit at the cemetery for the day. I decided to go to the cemetery early in the morning and allowed myself to cry there. I prayed for the strength to leave my grief there and move forward with a pleasant holiday.

On Michael's birthday a Catholic Mass was celebrated for him at our church. Mike's friends were invited to our home to celebrate his life.

I gave out wallet-sized photos of Mike and his deceased friend along with a medal of St. Michael, guardian angel. I provided a journal for his friends to write memories of Mike.

Our family, grandparents included, went to the cemetery together on Mike's birthday. We brought balloons, flowers, and music. We told stories about Mike. We laughed and cried together. Later that day we all went out for Chinese food, which Mike always loved.

Grieving is such a personal process, unique to each individual. I found comfort in reading, especially books related to child loss and spirituality.

There are times when I have a need to feel close to my son, though he is not physically present. When I am missing Michael most, I occasionally view videos of him. The experience is bittersweet. The tears may flow; however, seeing him smiling and laughing reminds me of how much he enjoyed life. It brings warmth to my heart.

Expressing my grief through writing by keeping a journal has been therapeutic.

Last summer I kept a plastic box with a journal at Michael's grave. A few visitors wrote nice messages in the journal; some brought a flower or other thoughtful items to the site. This has also given me comfort.

Grief has been like a ride on the roller coaster.

I've had more good days than bad since my second year. There are still days, however, when I'm feeling down and my pain feels so raw. My grief can still be easily triggered on some days. Just when I think I've moved beyond the anger and guilt, for example, something will trigger those emotions all over again. I'm grateful to the people I've met at The Compassionate Friends meetings. Many of them had experienced the same feelings which helped me to prepare for the ups and downs.

CHAPTER 3

Life changes

I do not believe that life on earth is guaranteed to anyone. I was given a wonderful gift for 19 years, and for that I am eternally grateful. I hold on to the hope that someday I will know the answers to the mysteries of life and that I will see Michael again.

Many people talk about letting go of your loved one. I don't think I will ever completely let go of Michael; however, my relationship with him has changed. I am working toward letting go of the pain associated with my loss, but it will take time.

I haven't made any major changes in the physical details of my life. I still live in the same house, work at the same job, and am married to the same man. The changes I have gone through are internal and go much deeper.

The death of your child changes you forever. How could it not? He was, and is, such an integral part of my life; and I wouldn't want to change that. I'm not the same person I was the day before he died. In fact, my life seems to be divided into two separate eras. It's like thinking in terms of BC and AD. The measure of time for me now is either before Michael died, or after.

The greatest change for me has been in the way I perceive life and death. I realize now that I used to take so much for granted. Life was something I felt quite secure about. I thought that life was guaranteed to my family, especially my children, until old age as long as we took reasonable care. I believed that God would always protect us and keep us safe from harm.

Before Michael died the passage of time seemed almost

imperceptible. I was busy living in my own world and didn't give much thought to the evolution of life. I now know that life isn't guaranteed to anyone. We are all vulnerable.

There are changes which feel uncomfortable. I've learned that life is fragile, and I feel less secure now. I no longer believe that only good things will happen and that we will always be safe. Life has lost its innocence for me. Feeling vulnerable is frightening. I hope that in time I will be able to regain a sense of security in life.

Some changes are good. I've become far more aware of how precious the gift of life is.

Now I am less apt to allow trivial things to bother me. I take time to notice sunsets, butterflies, small children laughing, and other gifts life has to offer.

I am always aware that life can be swept away in an instant. I just want to drink it all in. I treasure my daughter and my husband more than ever before. I try to hold on to all the blessings in my life for as long as I can. I am less apt to cling to material things. I believe I have a greater sense of compassion now, especially for grieving families. I have a desire to offer love and hope to others. I believe it is very important to communicate our love to those who are still present in our lives. We can't wait until they are gone, then it's too late.

I feel like I've gone through fire and reached a higher place. The pain is still there, and it humbles me.

During the third year of my grief journey I feel that I've made some progress. It has been a slow process; severe injuries need time to heal. I no longer sing to him or lie on the grass at the cemetery and cry. I seldom dream of death and loss now. I am able to think about my son with a smile and with warmth in my heart. I am able to talk about him without crying. In fact, I love to talk about him. Hearing Mike's name is like music to my ears.

I'm able to laugh and be in the company of friends more often without feeling like I'm pretending to have a good time. I feel like I'm moving closer to the eventual acceptance of my son's death while still keeping his memory in my heart and part of my life.

I'm working toward moving forward with my life. I believe it will be a long process. I've been able to clean out my son's bedroom and either give or store away all of his belongings. I'm proud of myself for that. I'm looking forward to the gift of grandchildren. Michael once wrote in a high school essay, "I am one who believes that every day should be lived to its fullest as though it is your last." I believe my son would want me to live fully, and that is what I plan to do.

What I would recommend to other grieving parents is to have patience. Allow yourself to grieve. I've discovered that people must grieve in their own way, even family members who have lost the same person. Don't put time limits on your grief. Ask for support from others if you need it, and don't be afraid to tell people what is helpful and what is not. Don't worry about what others think. Chances are they have no idea what it means to lose a child.

When you lose someone who is a large piece of the fabric of your being, you long to see him any way you can. Mike will always live in my heart, soul, and memory.

Since Michael died, I have had one vision and several dreams of him.

My first and only vision of Mike occurred less than one month after he died. My daughter, Kelly, and I were getting into my car one afternoon while searching for an apartment for her. I sat in the driver's seat. As I adjusted the rearview mirror, I had a visual image of Michael sitting behind me. I could see him so clearly. He had his head turned and was looking out the side window. I could see his facial expression, and even the clothes he was wearing. The image caught me off guard and lasted only a couple of seconds.

I've had many dreams of Michael since he died, especially during the first year. Most of the dreams were about death and loss; however, a few dreams have been very special and worth remembering. Having wonderful dreams about him leaves me with feelings of peace and love.

In one of my favorite dreams I lost my footing and fell off the side of a road leading to a steep cliff. I was hanging on to a rock and was afraid of losing my grip. As I looked up, I saw Michael standing safely on the road above me. Seeing my predicament he said, "Mom, get up!" I realized that I couldn't, and I asked for his help. He smiled, then reached for my hand and pulled me to safety.

One night I wrote in my journal that I wanted to have a nice dream of Michael. I was really missing him a lot, not just at the age I lost him, but at all stages of his life. That night I dreamed of him in many stages. We were in a room when he came to me as a toddler. We talked and hugged. He then left the room and returned a couple of years older. Again, we talked and hugged. This pattern continued through his teen years.

Recently, I had a nice dream on my wedding anniversary. In the dream Michael was a toddler, but I was aware that I would lose him in later years. He said to me, "Always remember that I will always love you." I was surprised in the dream that a toddler would say such a thing. I asked, "What did you say, Mike?" He said, "Never forget that I will always love you."

Some people say such experiences stem from direct communication from the person who died, but in a spiritual realm. I would like to believe that; however, the experiences have brought me peace and comfort.

Our children's mortality is something that we seldom allow ourselves to think about. The thought of the child predeceasing the parent just feels unnatural; it is something almost impossible to accept in our realm of reality.

There were two occasions in Michael's life when I briefly allowed myself to think about his mortality.

The first time was when he was 8-years-old. There was a period of time when Michael was having frequent headaches. I brought him to see the doctor who gave orders for him to be worked up. One of the tests ordered was an MRI of his brain. The doctor said we should "rule out the bad things first." This gave me cause for concern. I began to think about Michael's mortality.

During that period of time I recall once sitting on the sofa with him and saying, "Mike, if anything ever happened to you, Mama would cry for a hundred years." Michael looked at me with a smile. He then reached his arms around my neck for a hug and replied, "I love you."

The second time I considered Michael's mortality was when he was 18-years-old. He had joined the U.S. Marine Corps and was in boot camp. My husband and I went to the Marine base in South Carolina to see his graduation. I recall looking at Mike's dog tags, which revealed his blood type and religion. I shuddered as I thought about the reasons for having such information on the chain that a soldier wears.

I remembered back to the time when Mike was applying to be a Marine and he had to sign what seemed like hundreds of documents and consent forms. He later said to my husband, "Dad, I made you the beneficiary of my insurance policy." Perhaps we could have made light of the situation, but somehow I couldn't find anything humorous about it. Neither of us could have ever imagined we would someday need to make a claim against that policy.

I miss so many things about my son Michael. If I had to choose one thing, it would be his sweet smile.

When I think of him I remember his entire life, not just at 19-years-old. He was a very happy baby and had a joyful childhood. It was impossible to be depressed around him while he was growing up because he constantly made us smile or laugh. You really couldn't help but catch his spirit of life and joy. Once, when he was about four years old, we were in a dentist's office awaiting our turn. The room was quiet. Suddenly I heard Michael giggling with delight. I looked up from the article I was reading to see him standing alone in the middle of the waiting room floor. He had pulled out of his pocket one of those twirling things which falls from maple trees. He repeatedly threw it up in the air and belly-laughed as he watched it twirl to the floor. Soon I was laughing with him. I think about that little boy sometimes, and I can't help but think that's how life was intended to be for us all—laughing joyfully at life's little surprises.

Michael wanted everyone he loved to be happy. He was a sensitive, caring person. He never wanted to take anything I offered him if he felt that someone else needed it. He was loyal to his family and friends; he took every opportunity to enjoy life with the people he loved. He loved baseball and was a varsity catcher at his high school. He also loved classic cars and rebuilt a 1968 Firebird with his father.

Nov. 30, 2000, was one of the best days of my entire life. It was Parents' Day at Parris Island. That was the day before Mike graduated from Marine Corps boot camp. Steve and I hadn't seen him in twelve weeks, and we missed him terribly. Mike was so proud to show us his 'Expert' rifle, and eagle, globe and anchor pins, and to escort us around the base. Two days prior to his death he took me out for a special dinner. It was Mother's Day, and just the two of us were there.

When we arrived home from Baltimore, Mike's friends returned to our home. These grown boys wept bitterly as they told us that Mike was their "brother."

Approximately two weeks after Mike's death, Steve and I received notification that one of Mike's corneas was successfully transplanted into a "very grateful" 19-year-old. Knowing that Mike was able to give the gift of sight to someone he would consider a peer, filled the hole in my soul with awe. Two people received his heart valves. Because of Mike, others were given the chance to do as he had done, "live life to its fullest."

Mike has taught me so much. I will be forever grateful that he was in my life. He was a devoted son, brother, grandson, and friend. He is deeply missed by all who loved him. There will never be anyone quite like him.

PART II

Jane's Story
Christopher Lars Maki
Dec. 19, 1966—Nov. 5, 1997
Six Years Later

CHAPTER 4

A trail of blood

It was about 9 p.m. when officers from Lunenburg, MA, Police Department notified my husband, Ray, and me about our son, Chris.

Initially, the only information provided by our local police was that Chris had been found dead. We were given the name and telephone number of a Charlotte, NC, detective who filled in the horrendous details. I remember standing in the hallway while trying to absorb the full impact of what we were hearing, and recognizing that we were living a nightmare.

Those first few moments I had to acclimate myself to the reality that Chris was dead. It was both physically and emotionally traumatic.

Later, I called the Charlotte detective. He told us that on Wed., Nov. 5, 1997, our 30-year-old son, Christopher, was walking home from the South End Brewery in the trendy Dilworth shopping district of Charlotte. The streets were usually busy at the intersection of East Boulevard and Euclid Avenue, but at that early hour of the morning they were deserted as he headed toward his 330 East Kingston Ave. apartment. Chris had recently moved to Charlotte because of a job transfer.

Stabbed a total of 31 times, Chris died right there in the street, alone, within sight of his apartment.

Chris' body lay on the sidewalk for several hours. One passerby later told police they saw someone lying on the corner as early as 2:30 a.m. but dismissed him as a sleeping drunk. Another passerby on her way to work told police she noticed the body crumpled on the corner of East Boulevard and Euclid Avenue around 4:45 a.m.

Since he was robbed, police found no identification on his body. Even though Chris' wallet, identification, and credit cards were taken, police believed it was too soon to blame the killing on a robbery until they investigated further.

"We just don't know very much about why he was where he was" when he died, Investigator Steve Furr told the local newspaper.

It took investigators most of Wednesday to identify Chris' body using a piece of paper they found in his clothing. The more they investigated, the more they realized this was not a drug deal gone badly or anything like that; it was a random robbery that cost a decent person his life.

That was when they contacted the Lunenburg Police Department and asked them to inform us.

That night we were watching the second episode of The Lewis-Clark Expedition on PBS.

I had the book. I was totally engrossed in the program and following along with the book when the doorbell rang. That was, without doubt, the worst moment of my life. I have never been able to watch, read, or hear anything more about The Lewis-Clark Expedition. The book was stored out of sight and eventually given away. Today, even the mention of the name creates post-traumatic stress, and I immediately relive that awful moment.

I was never again able to put on the cozy, comfortable bathrobe I was wearing when we heard the news, which happened to be my favorite. That too was given away.

An autopsy had to be performed on Chris before his body could be sent home to Lunenburg. Because of this the calling hours would not take place until Sunday, with the funeral on Monday. During that time there was an endless flow of traffic in our home as family and friends tried to offer support and consolation.

While I was most grateful to everyone for trying to be there, I needed time alone. I would escape to the privacy and solitude of my bedroom where I would write and write and write. I needed to ventilate, and writing had always offered me that.

I noticed some behavioral changes following my son's death.

It revealed a side of me that I never knew. For example, the decisions about the calling hours and burial were not up for discussion. I knew what I wanted to take place, and there was no room for debate.

I had this compelling need to make the service meaningful and beautiful. While it was most uncharacteristic of me to do anything that would bring direct attention to myself, I announced that I wanted to speak at Chris' funeral. It was not something I had spent time thinking about. It was just a strong feeling of commitment; it seemed to be the right and natural course to take.

Police moved quickly. Frank Antrone Davidson, 32, of 2900 Burbank Dr., Charlotte, NC, was arrested early Fri., Nov. 7 and charged with murder and armed robbery. Two other suspects, both from Georgia, remained at large; however, it wasn't long before police arrested Frank William Mott, 41, of Hampton, GA, and Michael Neal McCall, 18, of Stockbridge, GA. They, too, were charged with murder and armed robbery.

The tip off was when the perpetrators tried to use one of Chris' credit cards.

Police believe what happened is these three men, high on crack cocaine, were cruising the streets of Charlotte when they noticed their car was running low on gas. They didn't have any money. When Chris' solitary figure loomed in front of their headlights, he seemed like easy prey. They came to an abrupt stop. One remained in the car sitting behind the steering wheel while the other two jumped out and attacked Chris.

During the initial struggle, Chris tried to defend himself, but he was stabbed multiple times. He was not a large person, only about 5' 5". A haphazard trail of blood stained the ground from East Boulevard and over the crosswalk telling the story of how he was able to free himself and run across the street where, in his weakened condition, he was chased down and overpowered. One of the men held him down while the other stabbed him. They rifled his pockets and took his wallet and any money they found in his pockets.

One thing I've learned to do is take comfort in whatever positive elements occur. Many homicides go unsolved. That is an added and ongoing pain for their loved ones. In our situation, Chris' murderers were captured and incarcerated within a week or two. Their sentencing was a year later.

We found ourselves dealing with the criminal justice system. There are times when the system does not seem just. Chris was dead. He had been attacked, robbed and stabbed to death, yet we were now involved in a process that seemed to be predominately concerned with the rights of the people who did this to him. How just is that? Yet, it is the system we live under.

Nov. 20, 1997, was our 32nd wedding anniversary. We will always remember that anniversary as the day we boarded the flight for Charlotte, NC, to deal with the murder of our son.

I remember feeling that this was all just a bad dream. Just a month before, we took that same flight to visit Chris and check out his new surroundings. We shared his excitement about the area. He was in a nice neighborhood, within walking distance of many restaurants and very near all the sporting arenas. He was so excited about an upcoming basketball game between the Boston Celtics and the Charlotte Hornets for which he had tickets. Now we were here again, but not to see Chris. We had to clear out his apartment and take care of his business affairs.

We had buried him at home; we felt like we were burying him all over again.

Friends and family had offered to clear out his apartment, but I could not consider that option. I did not want anyone to touch what he had touched: his pillows, his toilet articles, or the book he was reading still on his beside table. I needed to be the one to feel and touch anything and everything that Chris had touched. I needed to hold it all close to me, for it was as near to holding Chris that I would ever come again.

The two detectives working on the case met us in our hotel room the night we arrived. The detectives spent about three hours answering questions and informing us about the judicial process we would be dealing with in North Carolina.

I really liked both these men. They were courteous, respectful, and they made us feel that this was not just a case to them. In the course of their investigation they had read parts of Chris' journal and they were touched by the person he was. They assured us of their continued support and gave us their pager numbers. There was not one time when we called either of them that we did not get an immediate response.

When they were leaving, they both hugged me. One of them hesitated for a moment in the doorway. He turned and said, "For what it is worth, I want you to know that we see many murder victims who never knew what happened. Chris must have found his peace because he had the most peaceful expression on his face. I think you should know that."

Given the trauma we were continually experiencing over the circumstances of Chris' death, hearing that was truly a gift. There have been many times since that night when I have reminded myself of the detective's comment.

And that was the beginning of our new life.

On the day Chris was murdered, the life we had once known and loved died along with him. We were thrust into a new world, one that we had no knowledge of.

I knew the only way I could possibly survive each day was to keep Chris in it. Initially, I accomplished this by acknowledging the many expressions of sympathy that we received. It felt good to see how loved and respected Chris was. Responding was both time consuming and therapeutic. At first it seemed to be an overwhelming task; but once it was completed, I was left with a sense of emptiness and finality instead of relief and satisfaction.

I started a journal. I addressed the entries to Chris, and I wrote in it daily. It was here, in the privacy of my "Dear Chris" letters, that I was able to voice the anger, hurt, loss, confusion, and frustration which were now part of my daily existence. Chris had been the one to introduce me to writing in a journal. He had defined it as the best therapy ever. Here I was able to voice all my pain without ever having to hear the phrase, "move on." He alone knew the incredible feelings of hopelessness that consumed me. I allowed myself to feel that Chris was giving me his undivided attention as well as his permission to let it all go. This was my safe escape.

When I think back on the first year of life without Chris, I think of it as the beginning of the greatest challenge of my life—being able to live without one of my children. Each morning upon awakening I would wonder how I could possibly survive the day. Trying to take it one day at a time was too overwhelming; one hour at a time was struggle enough.

The month before Chris was murdered my brother broke both his feet in an accident. I became his means of transportation to and from work, and I continued to do that after Chris died. It was something I could do with someone I was comfortable being with. For quite a few weeks, it was the only reason I would leave my house. I think that was the single motivating force in getting me up each morning. Left alone, I would find myself crying uncontrollably. I did not think it was possible to cry as much or as hard as I did.

Much of the first year was like a blur.

If there was a single activity that prevailed during that first year it was probably that of an ongoing search: I needed to be in touch with other mothers who had survived the death of a child. Then I became obsessed with other victims, especially families who had been impacted by murder.

I read any book that offered hope or consolation. I kept trying to find something or someone who could ease my pain. I remember, for what seemed an eternity, waking up each morning to a nightmare. My family and I joined a support group called "Omega." It was a group specifically designed for families left behind who now had to deal with the fact that a loved one was the victim of homicide.

My husband and I faithfully attended the meetings for about two years. The contact we had with other survivors, along with the exposure to victim-related organizations and activities, became our lifeline and the beginning of a new way of life.

Confusion and restlessness were feelings I constantly struggled with. I did not want anyone around who would not or could not talk about Chris.

I found myself increasingly alone. Yet, when I was alone, I didn't know what to do with myself. One day my sister commented that I never called her. I knew she was feeling hurt because she was trying so hard to be there for me. I knew that in my own way I was shutting her out. I called no one other than my daughter because I did not know what to say, nor did I know what to talk about.

I was unable to think beyond Chris. I felt both helpless and hopeless. For the rest of the world life was moving on, and I didn't know how to cope with that. I was too busy trying to absorb the reality that Chris was really gone. He would not be home for the holidays or for any other day. He had been murdered. It was all a total, unbelievable nightmare.

On the fifth of each month I would routinely call our victim advocate in North Carolina. Although we had been assured that we would be informed of any and every development in the resolution of the case, this was my way of being visible and making sure Chris was not forgotten. I harbored the fear that Chris' case would not be a priority. Ours was not a high profile case in North Carolina, or any other place for that matter, except in the hearts of those who loved Chris. I saw myself as Chris' advocate.

On Nov. 10, 1998, the three men who murdered Chris were allowed to plead guilty to second-degree murder.

For the first time in my life I could understand what could lead a person to vigilantism. Our son had been robbed and stabbed to death by three men. I learned that this is where the victim is forgotten. It's all about what works best for the state, for the system, and in our situation that meant allowing a plea bargain.

North Carolina has the death penalty; and while I'm not an advocate of capital punishment, I did want to see them get the maximum penalty of life in prison. A plea bargain would not give them that. For many technical reasons, the district attorney felt that allowing them this option was the best course to take. If it were taken to trial, they would all be entitled to their own separate trials. Since there were no witnesses, there was the very real possibility that an element of doubt would creep in and any or all of them could be found not guilty. In fact, one of the accused had previously been tried in another murder case but was found not guilty.

Finally, after one long year, we were face to face with the three people who had stolen Chris' life and forever changed many others. They did not look like monsters, they looked like ordinary people; but they had done a terrible thing. Now they were standing in front of me, speaking through their lawyers about how they regretted their actions and how they had found Jesus Christ.

I made myself look at each of them. I would not take my eyes off them, yet today I couldn't tell you what any one of them looked like. I just remember thinking that they did not look like they were really hurting. I felt my heart rate accelerate and my head pound.

Only the 19-year-old's parents were in the courtroom. Other spectators present were one of my brothers, some people we had met through Chris' landlady, and the two detectives who had worked on the case. They had all come that day to offer their support.

I had told our victim's advocate that I intended to give a victim's impact statement. In retrospect, I don't recall considering that North Carolina might be one of the 20 states that do not allow this. I don't know what I would have done if that were the case.

Preparing and giving my impact statement became an obsession. I wrote and rewrote it more times than I can remember. It became a therapeutic tool. I wrote anytime I could, and many times at 3 or 4 a.m. Often when I found myself trying to formulate the many thoughts and feelings that I so desperately needed to convey, I was convinced that Chris was standing beside me, prompting me and enlightening me. I could almost hear him whispering, "Go for it Mom. You can do it."

CHAPTER 5

Impact statement

On that November day nearly one year after Chris was laid to rest, I had the only chance I would ever have to confront the murderers who changed our lives. Other than extreme anger, it's hard to recall what my feelings were as I looked at them. I remember frustration and feelings of helplessness as I realized I could do nothing to them that would in any way equal the pain we were enduring. I wanted them to really hurt for the rest of their lives.

I had no delusions that my statement would impact them, or that it would affect what their sentences would be, but that did not matter. All that mattered was that Chris would be actively represented. This was about Chris, not about the rights or the staged regrets of the accused.

When my moment came, I faced the perpetrators. Ray stood at my left; I was sure Chris was standing at my right. I began reading slowly, with clarity, so I would be heard.

"Your Honor, I appreciate this opportunity to speak. I would like to mention that in an attempt to be concise this statement was written by me in the first person. It does, however, directly reflect the feelings and sentiments shared by Chris' Dad, his brother Drew, his sister Amy, his family and extended family, our friends, and the many, many friends of Chris.

"When I was in college, I had a psychology professor who conducted her class in a non-traditional manner. We were never quite sure what her agenda would be.

"During class one day she made a statement that has had a

profound impact on my entire life. I have used it as a guideline for decisions that I have made throughout my adult life as well as for many of the principles that I have tried to instill in my children as they were growing up. They often knew what I was going to say before the words came out. That statement is this: 'In order to live a mature and responsible life, you must be prepared to make a decision, take the risk and pay the price.'

"In the past year, I have unquestionably felt the impact of that phrase more dramatically than at any other time in my life. Indeed, On Nov. 5, 1997, a decision was made, a risk was taken, and now the price is being paid by many. Despite the fact that we personally had no part in that decision making process, nor did we or Chris have any association with those who did, our lives have been permanently and dramatically altered; and the life we once knew and loved has ended forever.

"The primary victim was Christopher Lars Maki. He was, above all things, a beloved son, brother, grandson, nephew, cousin and friend. An energetic and conscientious worker, he was highly respected by colleagues and co-workers for many things, not the least being his intelligence, his integrity and his loyalty. Most of all, Chris was an inherently good and kind person who loved people and who formed deep and lasting friendships in the many places he lived, worked and socialized.

"He had not one enemy in the world. I never knew Chris to have a serious conflict with anyone… it was totally abhorrent to his nature. This is but a brief profile of the 5' 5", 30-year-old human being who, while innocently walking to his apartment, was attacked, robbed, stabbed 31 times and left alone to die in the early morning hours of Nov. 5, 1997. His funeral was on Nov. 10, 1997, exactly one year ago today.

"This was my first-born child, one of the true joys of my life. This was my beloved son."

I felt my body trembling as I looked at the three men who had murdered Chris and I continued to read.

"How and why did this happen?

48

"There is never a logical reason or answer to random acts of violence. We live in a world where violence is glorified, sensationalized, and often times excused. There is a lack of accountability for actions taken.

"One week ago we were here in this courtroom hopeful that there would be some resolve to this case. We were informed then that two of the defendants wanted to be able to discuss their sentencing options with their moms. How we would have liked it if Chris had been afforded the same consideration before receiving his sentence. Chris lived his entire life within the guidelines of the system. All that is left for him now is that the system be made to work for him. He deserves at least that much.

"My family and I are forever faced with an incredible loss, a pain and hurt that is beyond description. Each and every relationship we have has been affected. We are and have always been a very close family unit, and extended family, bonded by love and friendship. Each joyous occasion now is forever marked with the absence of Chris. He's gone. He'll never come home again.

"We are continually haunted by the vision of his final terrifying moments. This is an issue that I am particularly sensitive to. As a registered nurse for over 30 years, I am well acquainted with the dying process. Death is a natural and inevitable part of life for each and every one of us. However certain it is for us, there is also a basic, inherent fear associated with it. It is the fear of the unknown, the fear of being alone and perhaps even the fear of pain.

"It was not always easy to hold the hand of a dying person, to try in some way to make them comfortable. But it was always gratifying to know that in their final moments on this earth, my presence there was a source of peace and comfort to them and to their families. No one was there for Chris. No one held his hand.

"We wonder if he called out our names or if he felt much pain. Mostly we think of how terrified and lonely he must have felt. He died alone in a strange city for no reason other than he happened to be walking home at a time when three killers decided he was an easy target for something they wanted. They did what they set out to do, and then coldly and deliberately they moved on, never once glancing back.

"We are understandably frustrated and angry. Fighting this anger is a constant challenge and struggle. Not to someday meet this challenge would give you, his killers, a power that you do not deserve to have. We will not allow this to happen. Chris did not have the physical strength to win over you on that tragic November night, but we, his family and friends, are finding strength in our unity and our love and through the memory and the spirit of all that Chris was.

"There have been other victims as well.

"Your families and loved ones now must face the consequences of your actions. Their lives have also changed; their world will not be the same. They are forced to live with the knowledge that through the actions of someone they love an innocent young man's life was violently taken from him, and left behind are family and friends whose lives are tragically and permanently altered. Like us, they may have anger, loss, and frustration; but, unlike us, they still have hope.

"You are still alive. They can see you, speak to you, maybe even at some point they can hug you. I would give most anything for another one of Chris' hugs, or to pick up the phone and hear his, 'Hey,' as only he could say it, to once again hear the words, 'I love you Mom,' and that unique, infectious giggle that was so characteristic of Chris."

My voice cracked a bit, but by some miracle I did not cry.

"I have no idea what life will be for you now. Quite honestly, I don't care. You made a decision, you took the risk and, thank God, you are now paying a price, not enough of a price to be sure, but a price. Nothing will bring Chris back.

"Despite the limitations set upon you, you do have the option of choosing what direction your life will take from this moment on.

"There will someday be another verdict. In the end, you will be judged by the One who will judge us all.

"We are now left with only our memories. We cherish each and every picture we have of Chris, especially those taken at his sister's wedding. That was the last time he was home, the last time we were all together. There are his books, clothes, and special possessions of his that we cannot bring ourselves to part with. It is all that is left of Chris and when we do let them go, it seems to be as it really is, so very, very final. We do have many memories of the beautiful, blue-eyed, blond haired, happy little boy he once was and the honorable, loving, decent, and sensitive man that he became. We are enormously proud of that, we always will be. Nothing you have done, or may do in the future, will ever alter that.

"We are forever grateful for the gift, however short lived, of our Chris. He was small of stature, but so very rich in character. In the words of Chaucer's Prologue to The Canterbury Tales, '...he was a very gentle knight.'"

When I finished, all the tears I had managed to contain started to flow. I do not recall their reactions; I just remember being determined to get through it all with dignity.

My brother hugged me and told me how proud he was of me.

Ray was unable to speak. Watching the cold stare of one of the accused was more than he could handle. I had not seen him this distraught since the day our nightmare started.

One of the court officers approached me and told me how moved she was by what I said. The judge and district attorney asked for a copy of my statement.

I felt a sense of peace. I had done as much for Chris as possible, and I think he was proud.

We were prepared for the sentencing.

When the three men were originally charged with first-degree murder, prosecutors said they would push for the death penalty. But the plea bargain, allowing the defendants to plead guilty to a reduced charge, stopped a prolonged trial and restricted their right to appeal. The three men were allowed to plead guilty to second-degree murder and armed robbery charges. The district attorney had informed us earlier what the sentences were likely to be.

The judge almost seemed to apologize when he said that he was required by law to abide by the sentencing guidelines.

Frank Antrone Davidson, 33, of Charlotte, NC, will serve at least 26 years and 11 months.

Frank William Mott, 42, of Hampton, GA, will serve at least 22 years and 2 months.

Michael Neal McCall, 19, of Stockbridge, GA, will serve at least 18 years and 5 months.

The reason the sentences were different was because Davidson and Mott had previous criminal convictions.

Police said Mott and McCall told them they had robbed Chris to get money to buy drugs and go back to Georgia. Police said the suspects were tracked down because they tried to use the credit cards.

This has been very difficult for me to accept. I don't feel that anyone who has murdered another should ever be released from prison. I couldn't be satisfied with anything less than life without any chance of a pardon.

North Carolina does not have parole; however, once their term has been served, they must be released. I feel they made a decision, took the risk and should have been made to pay the price. I think 20 to 35 years in prison is too small a price to pay for their crime.

The youngest of the three was 18 at the time of the incident. He could conceivably be released before he is 40. Chris' life was cruelly taken from him. It was not an accident. It was not provoked. It was a deliberate act of violence.

The result was less than what I consider just, but the three men are now in prison and are unable to harm another innocent victim. I still feel incredible anger when I think of them. They're alive. They have certain rights beyond the basic ones of food and shelter. I'm sure they have cable TV and a gym. Most of all, they have hope. Thirty years can in no way compensate for the suffering we have endured; but, more importantly, it's much too small a price to pay for the beautiful life they took.

The moment I first realized that I was pregnant with Chris is one of those times that holds a very special place in my memory. For a very brief period, I alone shared a special private moment with the little life growing inside me. There were a few physical changes I was starting to experience, but it was the psychological ones that were the most profound. A life was growing inside me; I was going to be a mom. Ray and I were about to embrace that new world of parenthood. Our lives would now take on a new and beautiful meaning; one that we felt ready for and were anxiously waiting. We knew that things would never be quite the same again, and from this moment on we had to think beyond just ourselves.

Now, 30 years later, I thought back on that moment as I tried to process what was happening in our lives. It was as though life had come to a complete and abrupt halt. How ironic that the most wonderful change started with Chris' life, and now with his death we were facing the most challenging one.

The beginning of the rest of our lives commenced that Wednesday night, the worst night of my life. Minutes turned into hours, and hours turned into days.

I don't remember where one day started or where another one ended. It seemed to be just one endless nightmare.

CHAPTER 6

A life of dedication

I did not realize that I was developing a newfound assertiveness, some of which continues to be part of my life today.

Public speaking is by no means one of my talents. Yet, for something that is related to Chris and the circumstances surrounding his death, I will do now what a few years ago I would have considered unthinkable—speak in front of an audience of people. When a tragedy such as this happens, at least for me, there is a strong sense of commitment to try to raise awareness about the issue.

People say, "We would not wish this pain on our worst enemy." We live in a world where violence has become an acceptable part of life. It is glorified in our movies, present in many video games, and is a regular element of our nightly news. The horrendous realization of Chris' death as the direct result of another person's conscious, deliberate act has not diminished with the passage of time. This was not an accident, nor was it an act of God. This was a random act of violence.

The three men who murdered Chris needed money to support their drug habit. Chris' solitary and unsuspecting presence was their means to achieve that end. My objective is to impact people, especially young people, in understanding the total effect of the decision they made that night in performing that violent act. While one life was destroyed, many others are forever changed.

I hope that by sharing the personal aspect of my experience I can help create more awareness of society's responsibility in relation to violence.

Through it all, I believe Chris would want us to take this course. That is the basis of the Christopher Maki Memorial Foundation. He was a social, fun-loving kind of person who always believed in the basic goodness of people. It would be a betrayal of his life for us to live the remainder of our lives controlled by bitterness and anger.

I feel a negative change occasionally seep in. It is envy.

Until Chris was murdered I did not envy anyone. I remember riding with my husband one day and we were speculating about winning the lottery. While I would have welcomed some extra money, I never wished for the big one. I believed we already had the best that life could offer. We had a solid marriage, three great kids, a nice home, and a wonderful extended family. We were all healthy and happy. What more is there to need? I harbored the feeling that mega money would bring along mega problems. No one can have everything, nor is life meant to be perfect.

In a chance meeting with one of my friends, I experienced envy in a way I had never known.

This woman was thoroughly enjoying her retirement and her new role as a grandmother. At the time of our encounter, she was looking forward to taking a trip to visit her recently born grandson. I found myself obsessing and regressing to the "why me" stage again.

Life is going so well for some, but for my family and me it is such a struggle. I felt betrayed by the course our life has taken. In this instance we were two families who were bonded by years of friendship. We had experienced the growth and development of our children together; and we shared many of the same dreams, values, and ideals in life. Now, 20 years later, while one family has attained most of that dream, the other is trying to survive a nightmare. One family shares the photos and adventures of their offspring; the other seeks memorial contributions and support of their victim related causes. Beyond the discussions of shared times there is little left in common. It is difficult to spend any amount of time together on neutral ground because our lives have gone in such different directions. The dynamics of the relationship have changed. Now our times together occur less often.

Our friends have not changed, we have. Our situation and the resulting change in us is out of their comfort zone.

We all lived in a relatively safe community; and while there have been many tragic losses of young people, there have not been many murders. That is the unthinkable. Yet, if it could happen to Chris, why couldn't it happen to one of their own? My husband once defined our present situation as feeling as though we have leprosy.

I understand that our friends still care, but I feel that the comfort level they once experienced is harder to come by now.

For my part, I share their sentiments. I also care; however, I do not have the energy to act as though we are still the same people we were before Nov. 5, 1997.

We don't feel the need to have endless discussions about Chris or complain; but, our direction in life has changed. It creates another loss if we are not allowed to acknowledge or discuss some of those changes in a relaxed atmosphere with friends. One of our friends from the support group we participated in best expressed it with this simple phrase: "This is just the way it is; this is the way it is going to be, we have to learn to live with it."

For many people change is difficult. I believe the best thing people can do is try to make the most of their circumstances.

I have known people who have had severe losses and manage to go on with their lives while never looking back. I am not like that. Chris continues to be with me, and he will remain with me until I draw my last breath. It is difficult enough facing each day while knowing I cannot hear his voice or feel his hug, but to deny or ignore whatever presence I do feel for the sake of maintaining a friendship is unthinkable to me.

Every relationship we have has been affected.

Many friendships change over the course of time; but in most instances the change is gradual, mutual, and painless. Situations involving the loss of a child are different. Friends really feel helpless; they cannot make the pain go away. The very presence of parents who have lost a child serves as a constant reminder to others that no one is immune from tragedy. I sincerely believe that on a conscious level people really do try to be supportive on an ongoing basis, but the inability to see the quick fix or the happy ending is in itself depressing.

Each year during the Christmas season a group of graduates of the support group for survivors of homicide victims gather together. It is a small informal gathering. The group always lights a candle in memory of their loved ones, followed by a period of sharing. Last Christmas the group found it to be the most relaxing and needed event of the season.

Ironically, we spent very little time discussing our loved ones, but much time just talking amongst each other. Mostly, we just felt safe. It was comforting to know we were free to reminisce, or cry if necessary. Our children were not only present among us, they were an invited and welcomed presence; and it felt so very good being there.

Along with the loss of some relationships, there has been a formation of others. It is yet another change, but one that will hopefully assist us in our continuing quest to find peace.

In addition to facing life without one of our children, we have had to cope with the circumstances of Chris' death and the stigma often associated with it.

We felt compelled to defend Chris, who he was, and the fact that his death was the result of a random act of violence. Even today there are situations where we find ourselves defending him. Sometimes people say, "He was in the wrong place at the wrong time." It's an innocent cliché, often said with the best intentions. Yet, that statement implies fault on the part of victim, if he had not been where he was he would be alive.

Many times survivors of homicide victims are confronted with the dilemma of defending the circumstances of their loved one's death, even to people who should know better.

For example, while discussing the events of Sept. 11, 2001 with one man, he made the comment that what had happened to our son was awful; however, what happened to the September 11 victims we were speaking about was horrendous.

At the time I was so stunned by his remark that I was unable to respond. However, today I would tell him that other than the numbers involved, I fail to see any difference. While both were unsuspecting victims of an act of terror and violence, only one is considered a murder.

Something happened in our lives that fateful November morning that is irreversible. Life in general has changed immensely. The safety and security we once knew is gone forever.

I think any parent who loses a child faces unimaginable pain. To live life fully and productively is an ongoing challenge. I often feel as though a piece of my heart has been excised, and I must learn how to function without it. It is important to grieve whenever necessary.

Seeing a grief therapist has helped me cope with the vacillating emotions that I continue to experience. A support group opens the door to others who know your pain and have no expectations of how you should act. These are the people who really understand all the emotions and frustrations we encounter.

Often I think of those moments right before that fatal blow when, with no warning, for no reason, Chris was thrust into a world of violence, fighting for his life. Chris never fought with anyone. This was a world he knew nothing about. What confusion, panic, terror, and helplessness he must have endured.

This scene will play over and over in my head. While I never know what will precipitate it, or where I will be when it does happen, the effect is always the same. It is as if a piece of my heart is being ripped right out of me. I choke up and often hyperventilate. Anger that I never thought I was capable of consumes my every thought. It is difficult not to allow that anger more control over me than it already has. After all, our lives have been completely and cruelly altered in ways we could never begin to imagine before.

We are trying to adjust and cope with the ongoing pain and the changes each of us have endured. Why Chris? Why us? What have I done for God to punish me in this way? Is there really a God, and where was He when Chris needed Him?

This is the ultimate pain; there can be none worse. It will never be over. It may lessen, but it will never go away. A life is gone forever, so what is this closure thing all about? Do we pretend he never lived, or do we just not think about him? How do we attain closure?

Grief is not something our society is particularly comfortable with; it does not do well in this environment. It is tolerated for a brief mourning period. We live in a quick fix society where there is a fast solution to everything. People want to know that we are healing and moving on, and that there has been closure. When you lose a child, there is no closure, ever.

The first Christmas after Chris was murdered my twins gave us a beautiful oil lamp. This lamp burns on many occasions but it burns almost constantly from October 31 through Christmas.

I suppose I think of that time as my own mourning period. It encompasses so many special or significant dates. October 31 was the last contact I had with Chris; Thanksgiving was always the day that our immediate family and extended family celebrated at our home. Perhaps it is for that reason it ranked as his very favorite holiday. His birthday was on December 19, and Christmas was always our own special family day as well as my birthday. We would spend the entire day just enjoying being together and sharing our gifts with each other.

Each year we commemorate the anniversary of Chris' death by having a Mass said. Usually we follow the service with a potluck supper in our home.

We send out invitations to our family and to many of our friends. It feels right because Chris really loved people and he looked for any opportunity to get people together. This gives us the opportunity to celebrate his life with those who loved him and those he loved. We always burn a candle by his picture at home as well as one at the cemetery.

We established the Christopher Maki Memorial Foundation as a memorial to Chris. The mission of the foundation is to educate everyone about the occurrence and consequences of violence.

Each spring we have a walk in our community. Proceeds from the walk benefit our scholarship program for high school seniors as well

is' Crusade: A violence prevention program offered to area
e school students.

I know that as long as I live Chris will be an active part of my life.
I will never let go of him. Involving myself in his foundation, as well
as in other victim related causes, has allowed me the opportunity to
direct my energy in a positive way and hopefully to promote the
causes Chris would be a part of. Many times when I engage in these
activities I think his spirit is beside me. That is where I get my
strength.

When Chris started college in the fall of 1984, we had an old trunk
he used for his belongings. Before he left we all wrote a message on
the inside of the cover. In big letters we wrote,"Make us proud Kip,"
and we all signed it. I like to think Chris is now giving me that
message and he is indeed proud of the course my life has taken during
the six years since his murder.

Now, six years later, I do not write in my "Dear Chris" journal
regularly. Sometimes I feel guilty about that. I realize it's more a
matter of time rather than neglect.

I write about Chris in other ways. He continues to be as much a
part of my life as he ever was. Working in groups with other
survivors of homicide victims and being involved in projects and
activities to curb violence and create education and awareness are
my positive ways of keeping Chris with me.

One of those projects is The Garden of Peace, a memorial to
victims of homicide built in Boston. Originally conceived by
members of Parents of Murdered Children, support has since
broadened into a statewide coalition of groups, individuals and
public officials committed to creating an appropriate memorial to
homicide victims. It is intended to serve as a special place where
individuals can remember and celebrate the lives of their loved ones
which were ended by violence.

Designed by two local artists, Catherine Melina, a landscape
designer and Judy Kenley McKie, a sculptor and herself the mother
of a homicide victim, the garden reflects various stages of grief,
healing and hope. The cast bronze sculpture is designed to depict

three ibis ascending. The ibis is a heron-like bird that was considered sacred to the ancient Egyptians. It represented their god, Thoth, who was the god of wisdom, healing, love and truth. It was also the symbol of resurrection.

The journey from grief to hope is represented by a dry river bed with homicide victims' names engraved on smooth river stones. Along the way, the dry river bed turns into a trickle of water, like possibilities returning. The memorial also includes seating along the walls and a gathering place for public assemblies.

Along with many dedicated volunteers, our daughter Amy and I have both been actively involved in this project. Although time consuming and often overwhelming, the garden and Chris' foundation help give my life purpose by allowing Chris an active part in it.

That Chris was with us for 30 beautiful years is a gift that I will always be grateful for. I think that Ray, Drew, Amy, and I have bonded even more as a result of all that has happened. Recently we purchased a campground together in the White Mountains area of New Hampshire. This is a family business venture that we all feel very good about and we know Chris is a part of. He loved skiing in New Hampshire; the fact that we found this property almost without looking is more than a mere act of fate. Added to this, the stones with the victims' names for the riverbed at the Garden of Peace were all taken from this property. I cannot help but to feel that Chris has had a direct part in all of this.

As time goes on I miss Chris more and more. The reality that he will never come home again is beginning to set in and it hurts. I miss his one or two line e-mails. I miss his Sunday night telephone calls and hearing his voice saying, "Hey, what's up?" I miss his infectious giggle, his special trips home, and his shoes under the kitchen table. Most of all, I miss all that he was and all he wanted to be. I look forward to that day when he greets me with a great big smile and an enormous hug. One of my favorite quotes written by Thomas Campbell in The Hallowed Ground is, "To live in hearts you leave behind is not to die." Chris continues to live on in our hearts. He will never die.

PART III

Deborah's Story
Peter John Kulkkula
April 27, 1974—September 23, 1993
Ten Years Later

CHAPTER 7

Forever changed

In August 1993, my husband, Peter, and I returned home with our 19-year-old son, Peter John, from a trip to visit our daughter, Jane, in Washington State.

Just as things were getting back to normal, I received a telephone call at work from my husband on my private line. I couldn't understand what he was saying because he was hysterical. The only words that I could make out were "Peter John."

Since I had clients in my office, I excused myself and took the call in the empty lobby where I picked up the reception telephone. As we began to talk, more clients entered the lobby.

"What about Peter John?" I asked, shaking.

His reply was that Peter John had been in a bad accident.

"Okay! Okay! Where is he? Is he being operated on?" I asked.

My husband was barely audible. He couldn't seem to get the words out. More clients walked in. I was hoping that some were for my partner. By then I was becoming aggravated with my husband because he was putting me in an awkward position.

I straightened my body, controlled myself and said, "Honey, just tell me what hospital Peter John is in and I'll meet you there."

My husband's voice got a little stronger. He said Peter John was at home and the police, fire, and ambulances were there.

I looked around and saw more clients had entered the lobby. They were all quiet. They seemed to be listening to my conversation.

"All right," I told him. "You go to the hospital with him and I'll meet you there."

Peter seemed to be choking on his words. He said that the ambulance wasn't bringing him anywhere.

At that point, I demanded, "Let me talk to Peter John."

My husband broke down again. He said that Peter John couldn't come to the phone because he was dead.

I gasped for air, not believing what I heard. I felt so weak that I leaned on the reception desk. Then I gathered the strength to ask, "What did you say?"

This time, Peter clearly stated that our son was dead.

Now it was my turn to say it. "Peter John is dead?"

"Yes. Peter John is dead." he said. All the clients were watching me.

I finally asked, "Where will they take Peter John now?"

It took him a long time to make me understand that he didn't need to go to the hospital. The funeral home director would pick him up. I begged him to keep Peter John at home until I could see him.

Everyone in the outer office and lobby was quiet. I'm sure all of them heard me. I managed to apologize. They just seemed stunned.

My husband said that he'd come to get me.

"No, you're too upset to drive," I told him. "I'll come right home. Keep Peter John there until I get there."

I pushed my weight off the desk and held the wall as I walked to my secretary's office. I opened the door, and then held onto the doorway with both hands. I tried to tell her in my best professional voice to cancel the rest of my appointments.

"Why?"

"Peter John died."

At first she thought I was joking.

Then she realized that I was telling her the truth. I was able to tell her what to do with my clients and that I'd wrap up the business in my office and go home. As I began to deal with my clients, my secretary came in and asked them to reschedule with her so I could go home. She was practically pushing me out of my own office. She told the clients what had happened. One of the people in the lobby said that she would bring me home. I was coherent enough to tell her how to get to my house.

I couldn't feel. I couldn't believe it. I remember saying, "It just can't be."

I remember arriving home and getting out of the car.

I could feel death in the air. My house was surrounded by police cars, fire trucks, ambulances, and onlookers. Then, from out of the sea of people, my pale-faced, red-eyed husband appeared running toward me with outstretched arms. I dropped my purse and fell into his arms. Our tears bonded us in a hurricane of grief.

Finally, my lips formed the words, "Where is Peter John?"

Peter John had been working in our old horse shed, which he had converted to a work area. My husband pointed to a very awkwardly jacked up car. The car had fallen on our son as he was installing a transmission.

He had died suddenly and alone.

There he lay; pale, gray, almost white, without any sign of his warm nature, big innocent eyes, or the smile that always made me return one. His hands lay dormant, never again to hold someone else's hand.

I reached out to him, but my husband held me back saying it was unsafe. My husband, seeing how distraught I was, asked if I could please to go to our son. The police officer's answer was "No."

I begged the emergency personnel. "I have to hold him one more time," I told them.

One fireman replied, "I think we can secure it for you." They all nodded at each other. Once it was safe, I was allowed to kneel in the dirt beside my son.

I held his cold body in my arms as my husband held me in his. His cold lifeless lips would never eat lobster, pizza, or ice cream again. They would never form the words 'I love you,' or give away kisses any more. Never more would he mow the lawn by tying the lawn mower to his dirt bike, plow the yard with a door tied to the front of his van, or tell us that his new car was cooler than ours.

It was in that moment, holding our son's lifeless body while my husband held my sobbing body, that my life forever changed.

I would never be the same person that I was before. My life

suddenly divided into two parts: before and after Peter John's death. Right after Peter John's death the house seemed to be veiled in a burdensome, dark mist that almost choked me. The only thing that broke through the fog was a horrible sound, the sound of soft, grief-stricken chatter, which seemed like yelling in my ears. I had to make excuses to leave so that I could endure doing what had to be done for Peter John.

My husband Peter and I left our family and friends behind as we attended the grim task of going to the funeral home to pick out a casket for our son and to make arrangements for his final resting place at the cemetery. We held hands as we walked. It felt as though my body was detached from my consciousness. I was in another place, looking at myself walking with my husband while choosing the cemetery plot.

One final thing we did was stop at a store for waterproof mascara for the calling hours and funeral. It was so strange watching myself making these kinds of decisions. I felt like a hollowed out person, shaking and hanging onto my husband to keep myself upright.

For the funeral, family members chose the music and Peter John's sister, Jane, picked out a music video that concluded with a dove flying toward heaven.

The dove became my symbol for Peter John. That first year, I kept buying little dove pins and handing them out. I invited everyone to wear one in loving memory of Peter John.

My family decided that I should give the eulogy, which I did. I was very surprised when my husband Peter decided to speak, too. Surprisingly, when we invited others to share their memories of Peter John, they generously did.

My husband and I were glued to each other. We could not stand without the support of one another.

Peter and I had taken time off from work. We thought we were grieving, now we know we were in shock. We couldn't believe our son was dead. I literally went from experiencing the world with no feeling, to being filled with so much emotion that it overflowed with great waves of tears. In addition, I had an immense need to share my feelings and story.

We both went back to work after a week. We attempted to continue our routines; however, our minds, emotions, and bodies didn't allow this. It hurt so much it was nearly unbearable. I had to shut down my feelings in order to cope.

Emotionally, I felt like someone had decimated my heart, and then gave it back to me with an irreparable gaping hole which could never be mended.

At the cemetery, I was barely able to lift my right foot as I stepped on the grass near my son's grave. Then I dragged my left foot forward. My whole body seemed to be weighted down as I fell to my knees hugging my son's grave.

On my return to work I found it hard to concentrate. I was just going through the motions. My planning skills were gone. Sometimes I would find myself being vacant, not doing or thinking anything.

I was in rough waters, but I found that I did have a choice. I could either get caught up in the tidal wave of denial, guilt, and bitterness; or I could use my grief voyage in a positive manner. I chose the latter.

I came to learn that the high seas of the grieving process were filled with rough waves, and calm ripples. When I least expected it, I was hit with tidal waves of inconsolable grief for my son.

I begged my daughter to come home, telling her that I needed her.

I had dropped off the vacation film from our trip to visit Jane in Washington State. Shortly after the funeral the prints needed to be picked up.

I brought them home and dropped them on the dining room table. There were so many envelopes. I asked myself if there was any reason to open them. Did I really want to see how happy we all were just a couple weeks before? Then I wondered if the lobster dinner photos were there from just two Sundays ago. Peter John and his friend had enjoyed the lobster so much. They had been fooling around with the claws. I think that was when I got the camera going.

"Oh well," I thought, "I don't want to see them. Who cares? I don't have Peter John, so who cares?" They sat there for about a month, and then I put them in a box and moved them from place to place until one day, when I tried to dust off the top of them, the box dropped and the envelopes got all mixed up.

Since I had originally put the films in the envelopes in chronological order, I put them in numerical order. Here was the last one. Was it the lobster dinner film? I slowly pulled the tab up. It looked like all of the photos came out. Then, I put it back into the box. Every few days I picked it up again.

One day, my need to see the photos overtook me. As I looked at the photographs I began to smile. They were beautiful.

The boys had enjoyed a wonderful meal that night. Looking at the photo with the lobster claws on their noses, my eyes welled with tears. Teardrops hit the photo, one by one.

I looked through the photos and reprinted many to make albums for family members and Peter John's friends. I added many other photos and distributed them. Then I couldn't stop. I treated all my family to professional photographs because I wanted them to have current photos of themselves and, of course, one for myself. By now, I was surviving from day to day on photo projects. It took two years before I could really look at Peter John's baby or childhood photos. At that time I made reprints of some of them for family members.

By the second month, I was so desperate and full of pain; I was ready to get into the grave with my son.

I was depressed. I felt helpless and hopeless. Even though I wasn't suicidal, I was careless about my own personal safety. I wouldn't lock doors or buckle my seat belt. I would drive too fast.

I don't think anyone can lose a child that they dearly love and not be depressed. My husband and I both were suffering deeply from the loss of our son.

My husband often held me and we cried together. I think my crying, and his need to take care of me, gave him permission to cry too.

During the first few weeks, I cried constantly. Crying was a way to release the sorrow I was feeling. As I write this, 10 years later, I still cry occasionally. If I go to a wedding and think about Peter John, and imagine what a good husband and father he would have been; or, if I'm shopping and see a man helping a woman who appears to be his mother, I'll cry.

At first I felt nervous, empty, shaky, and panicky. I had lots of aches and pains. My weight dropped to 103 pounds by that first Christmas. When my daughter came home for the holidays she scolded me about my weight.

I felt I had lost control of my life and didn't know how to get it back. I needed kindness, patience, and understanding. I have found that the ever changing nature of grief is specific to each individual. How I may have reacted could very well be different for someone else; however, no matter how one copes, the loss of a child changes that person's life forever.

Peter and I had a lot of difficulty sleeping. We tried many things, even buying a new mattress. Finally, after three months, we found something that worked; it was some music to play for an hour before bedtime. The music, along with our new mattress and the aid of a prescription from our doctor, finally gave us some relief so that we could sleep for a few hours a night.

Peter John's three remaining grandparents all asked God, "Why not me?" I, a devoted Christian, did not ask that question; however, I did bargain.

I had asked God what I could do to change things. He did not reply until I asked Him for the strength to help my family and me through our loss.

I also bargained with God about being able to be sure that Peter John was all right. I just wanted and needed some sign. I decided to be open to seeing them. Once I did this, signs were abundant. On Sept. 27, 1993, the day of the funeral, there was a blossoming of an Easter lily. Flowers began to pop up early in our yard the next year on Peter John's birthday. There was a rose that bloomed on the anniversary of his death. Whenever my husband and I saw a rainbow we felt that it was a message.

But I believe I had an actual visitation from Peter John in early February 1994.

I awoke that morning and heard someone in my kitchen. I got up and found Peter John there. He was making a sandwich. He smiled and gave me a great big hug and told me he loved me.

I said, "I love you too, honey." I asked him, "Why didn't someone tell me that you were all right?"

He replied, "No one else could do it, Mom."

I kissed him again. I looked into our family room at the couch. No one was there. Somehow I thought that it confirmed that he had risen and was alive again. I turned back toward him. He lovingly bear hugged me and said, "Mom, I'm okay."

I was thrilled that he was alive. I said, "Thank God!" I went into the bedroom to wake my husband, and then Peter John was gone. It started to sink in. He was all right, but he was not alive.

I don't know if this was a dream, a vision, or really him. I know God was aware that I needed to know that he was all right. The strange nightmares I'd been having about dead people being packed in ice stopped that day. I think that morning there was a new dawning for me, but also for Peter John, his sprit was free.

Intellectually, I understood Peter John was dead the moment I held his body in my arms. What I didn't understand was the enormity of the loss. Our son's missing place at the table was almost impossible to bear. First denial, then anger, and eventually, with unrelenting anguish, I came the realization that our son was gone.

I needed to know I wasn't crazy, that help was important, that I would gradually resume normal activities, that the intolerable pain I felt would become bearable.

CHAPTER 8

Only positive memories

There were many "what ifs."

At first I was feeling good that I had bought Peter John a hydraulic jack. Then one day while driving home I realized that he had used two hydraulic jacks on the day he died. I regretted getting him just one. If I had bought two, he wouldn't have used the older one.

In retrospect, I believe going back to work was good for me. It protected me for a few hours everyday during those first few months.

Some of my memory and critical thinking skills seem to have been short-circuited. Before my son's death I received two masters' degrees with 4.0 averages. Now, I can't develop a curriculum plan without the help of notes; write without a spell checker; and I can't go to the grocery store without a list.

I remembered all the unselfish, loving things that Peter John had done for us. I laughed about the naughty things he had done too. Now they seemed unimportant. There are only positive memories about Peter John.

Our daughter, Jane, was a perfect child. We gave her all we could. But our son was adventurous and prone to accidents. My husband and I decided to show Peter John responsibility by making him work for everything: date money, driving lessons, his first car, and his own car insurance. He even had to pay most of his college expenses. I regret that. If I had known, I would have given him everything I could. Basically, I would have tried to make his short life full of fun.

I regret my son died alone. I regret not being able to say goodbye. When Peter John died I tried to cling to my daughter for fear something might happen to her. As an inner city missionary, she often faced dangerous situations. I wanted her to come home. I thought that would make it better for all of us. This pushed my daughter to end her mission before she was ready. She came home and began to grieve. She was different. She didn't smile. She couldn't decide what to do next. It wasn't any better for me or for her.

I guess I expected more from the people around me. I thought we had reached out to so many people prior to our son's death that people would reach out to help us. The lack of support was disappointing.

During the first year, events—holidays, special occasions, death anniversaries—were dreaded and very difficult.

Peter John's monthly anniversary was always a sad day. Now, 10 years later, it still can be painful, yet there are times when we are okay.

The first anniversary was very difficult. We set up a service at the graveside.

Finally, well into the first year, I blamed God. There really was no other place to put my anger. Shortly after that, I asked God for forgiveness, and I feel He gave it to me.

Emotionally, my world became unstable. I could trust nothing. I was afraid for everyone around me. If Peter John could die, maybe one of them could also die. Physically, at one moment I felt like I was standing on unsteady ground, and the next moment I felt like I was on solid ground, and then it would become shaky again. I had to hold onto something to keep from falling.

Without God's help, I would not have survived.

My husband and I married young. Neither of us had lived as adults without the other. Even as we grew, and our dreams and desires changed, we accepted the changes, and helped each other through our journey.

We enjoyed having our family. Our house was filled with love. Peter made it possible for me to stay home while our children were growing up. He helped at home whenever he was needed even though he worked long hours.

I began to see the signs of my husband's grief. His face would become pale and his eyes would fill with tears. I would touch his arm as we drove, hug him at home, and take his hand to show him that I understood his pain.

This earth-shattering experience put a great strain on both of us. We could have given up on our marriage, but we chose to work at strengthening it.

I felt that if my family could come together and support one another we would be able to handle things. I was wrong. I needed to understand that we would all grieve differently and that we would not be in the same stage at the same time. Grief comes in waves; none of us would ever be able to anticipate what any of the others would be feeling on any given day.

Much traveled, Peter and I stayed close to home after Peter John's death. However, after three years, we began to travel again in memory of Peter John.

In the first year, we spent a lot of time and money that might have been better spent elsewhere if we had waited until the storm of grief had subsided.

Our daughter finally returned from Washington State, but things had changed. She was not the same person she was before her brother's death. She had to face his death. She had to begin her grief process. Jane wanted her brother's room. Later on, she's the one who started to really clean it out.

This must have added to her pain, and she decided to move. Eventually she met the man who would become her husband. She is a whole person again and as happy with her life as she can be after losing her brother.

I often felt that I went back to work soon after my son's accident because it was a place for me to hide from what had happened.

I couldn't stay home. Home really isn't the right word for it because it was more like a tomb: that was where our son was robbed of his life. A damp, dingy smelling darkness took over our home and yard. It felt like a graveyard. By going to work, at least I was with the living. Work required me to turn my feelings off.

I think that was good. However, it became more and more difficult for me to deal with people. Three months later, I quit my job and stayed home to take care of my husband and his mother.

Peter and I have been on a mission. We have thrown ourselves into projects dedicated to Peter John.

We coped by keeping our son's name alive. We tried to do projects that would honor Peter John. In addition, we tried to tie his name to as many of these projects as possible. Every time we see our son's name connected to one we feel good.

The first year our church dedicated our Crop Walk for world hunger to our son. Peter John had been part of it since he was a baby being pushed in a carriage. He was the youngest walker when he was only four. My husband and I worked hard to make this walk our most effective one.

We knew our son would have a lot of flowers, so we asked people to send money to our church's youth fund. The financial leaders of the church decided that the money would go into the scholarship fund. Many people sent checks to the fund. We submitted all the checks that were sent to us. The fund's name was changed to the Peter John Kulkkula Scholarship Fund. These scholarships are given out in January and June.

As other church members passed away, their families asked that people send donations to our son's scholarship fund. I watched the obituaries so my husband and I could contribute and thank the families.

Peter and I decided to give an annual scholarship at Peter John's high school. The Peter John Kulkkula Memorial Scholarship Award is presented to an average Fitchburg High School senior who excels in creativity or ingenuity in art or writing. Both the Art and English departments are encouraged to nominate students who excel in one or both of the suggested areas.

We present the check, a certificate, a graduation card, and a rose or pen to the scholarship winner at the school's award ceremony. We may cry when we give it, but we feel refreshed by the time we leave the school. Whenever we have a chance to get Peter John's name out there, we feel that we have kept his memory alive.

My husband and I worked on and donated to several causes in memory of our son. A small one was the nametags in memory of our son for various organizations that we belong to. Among the substantial ones were donations to the Fitchburg State College Alumni Fund and The Compassionate Friends in loving memory of Peter John.

Reaching out to others had always been a part of my life. That did not change.

At first, I could not reach out to someone else because I was hurting too much. But later on, after I learned to accept and live with my own grief, I could begin to reach out to others. A year and a half into my grief, I was helping others.

I could do this because others had reached out and nurtured me in my struggle. I received that help from a group called The Compassionate Friends, an international self-help organization for bereaved parents and siblings. In their mission statement they say that they offer understanding and friendship to aid parents and siblings in the positive resolution of grief for their child or a sibling, and to foster both the physical and emotional health of the individual.

I began to go to The Compassionate Friends meetings in early January 1994. We met in the basement of a church and the room was cold; however, the people I met there warmed me. The people at The Compassionate Friends meeting reached out to Peter and me as though we were their own family. They helped us through our grieving. The Compassionate Friends remained steadfast in helping us throughout the first few years of our bereavement.

I began to go to meetings regularly. I felt safe and comfortable, and I was able to share my feelings. They helped me realize I wasn't crazy. They showed me they were there for me to lean on. Most importantly, they understood what I was going through.

That was where I heard about a highway island that one mother had sponsored and dedicated in memory of her son. I thought that sounded like a good idea. I called city hall and they told me which ones were remaining. They were all big. I took the one that I thought would be most visible.

My husband helped me clean it up. Remembering Peter John's love for roses, we planted rose bushes on the island. We brought fertilizer and water to the island and tried our best to care for the roses. They had a hard time with the constant exhaust fumes from passing traffic. Then, people told us that the rose bushes would not survive the winter there because of the road salt. I panicked. I dug them up and brought them home. I put them in my cellar, keeping a light on them. I watered them and took them out in the spring with only two left.

We planted annuals for a couple years. But now we have various hardy evergreen bushes.

Ultimately, we became more involved in The Compassionate Friends. They helped us by allowing Peter and me to reach out to help the newly bereaved by encouraging us to be meeting hosts, then meeting coordinators, and eventually meeting leaders. When we became more seasoned at helping others, we became the leaders of our chapter.

Just after we got involved with The Compassionate Friends, we attended a regional conference. With my background in educational leadership, I went to a couple of the leadership seminars. I was also interested in the chapter newsletter, so I went to the newsletter seminar.

In the mid-1990s my husband and I wanted to find out more about The Compassionate Friends leadership so we went to the International Conference in Nashville, Tenn. My husband and I have been the leaders of our chapter since the late 1990s. More recently, there was another regional conference we attended, and we encouraged our members to attend. In the summer of 2000 we went to The Compassionate Friends leadership training in Delaware where we got a broad view of chapter leadership.

Other people needing grief counseling began to come to me. I really believe they thought that I had some magic elixir to help them get through their tragedy. I tried my best to help by being patient and kind; but most of all, I listened.

CHAPTER 9

The Compassionate Friends

After my first year with the group I did a few newsletters a year. The senior editor helped me learn. She taught me what I needed to know and where to find helpful material.

The following year I became more involved and eventually became lead editor. The responsibility was mine. I matched editors with jobs that they could do. A year or so later, I became the senior person and eventually guided the other two editors with other much needed work for the local chapter.

For several years I edited, published, and even printed the newsletters myself. I gave up the job as newsletter editor when we had volunteers for research, typing, and proofreading editors.

Now we have taping, research, and text editors. The process hasn't worked perfectly yet; however, over time, I feel confident it will. With the new organization, our newsletter editors seem to get support from each other by phone and email. As leader, I still am responsible for getting the general chapter material. But there are others who have important roles: our meeting leader coordinator, meeting host coordinator, data base manager (birthdays and anniversaries), treasurer (love gifts), librarian (book news), as well as our chapter members (poems, stories, and articles) all submit material to the new editor. We have a newsletter printing person who prints the newsletter on a Rizzo high-speed copy machine.

The newsletter for the local chapter of The Compassionate Friends has a bulk mailing of almost 500. When I took over the leadership, I was given that job as one of my responsibilities. I had to learn how to do a bulk mailing and then teach a group of members of The Compassionate Friends how to do it. This group meets bimonthly to prepare the newsletter for mailing and to support one another.

It can be therapeutic for the newly bereaved if they want to help the chapter. I found this to be a place to chat informally with the others. We help each other in our grieving process.

One newly bereaved mother told me that I was her inspiration to go on. I'm glad that my work to help other parents wasn't in vain. I remember Nancy, who patiently helped me take over the chapter responsibilities. She was my inspiration. I was just completing the circle of compassionate caring that Nancy had started.

The time came when the group needed to find a new meeting location. Another church volunteered to help us out. Now we meet in a larger and warmer room.

The new church supports our mission by providing both a meeting space and coffee supplies.

Recently, a newly bereaved mother came forward with a great need to help. I have met with her and other newly bereaved folks, about various publicity ideas and about a chapter flyer.

If we start a project, we will probably finish it. There are times when the clouds in our minds clear and the sunlight comes through. Those are the times we get ideas.

In one of those bursts of sunlight, I often wonder what needs to be done, and how we might strengthen The Compassionate Friends. One thing that remains clear to me is the need to continue the mission, and to reach out to newly bereaved parents with care and kindness.

It has become very difficult to contact the newly bereaved individually because of the recent Federal Privacy Act legislation.

We must develop new methods to tell them about The Compassionate Friends. Our publicity campaign has become vital. We've developed a small public relations group to help with this effort.

The Compassionate Friends has helped me and continues to do so. It is my privilege to reach out to others and help them. The support

I have received through The Compassionate Friends can be described as a circle of sharing, caring, and helping.

After I had been with The Compassionate Friends eight years, a small group met and wrote a pamphlet to help newly bereaved parents.

The support each member of that group gave the others almost equaled the importance of producing the booklet. The feelings we have for each other still goes on. After a recent loss, the newest bereaved person in the group, who really needed our writers support group, sent me a lovely note.

And then, after nine years, another group of The Compassionate Friends shared authorship with this book. We all agreed that writing this book has helped us all to move along on our own grief journey. The caring brought us closer. We were bonded by our compassion for one another and in our mission to reach out and help others.

I began to speak at local grief conferences a few years ago.

I'm an enthusiastic speaker. But, speaking about my grief experience still occasionally brings a quiver to my voice. Because of the recent Federal Privacy Act, I really feel that we all need to get the message to all newly bereaved parents and their families that The Compassionate Friends exists for them. Public speaking is a way to do that.

The greatest change since Peter John's death has been my focus.

In my early adult years, I cared for my children, Jane and Peter John, my foster children, my husband and many animals.

I sponsored over twenty Vietnamese boat people with the help of other members of my church. Then when one refugee, Quy, needed a home, Peter and I became his legal guardians. We became Quy's parents in all the ways that count. In those days, my family was my identity and life.

As my family grew up I went to college and received four degrees and two educational certifications. I taught third and fourth grades and instructed college students to teach those grades. My specialty was participatory learning. In 1991 I wrote a manual on participatory learning that was sold to many schools throughout the East Coast. I was just getting established as a leading educational specialist when Peter John died. This terrible tragedy changed my entire life.

After Peter John's death my direction in life turned back to family. I needed to take care of them. Now, I found myself caring for three generations. My mother-in-law needed constant care, my parents needed help, my husband, daughter, Jane, and, Quy needed love and care. I threw myself into helping them in the same way that I had when I was a young mother.

I handled my grief by rebuilding my life.

After Peter John's death I knew two things: I could never teach children or college students again, but I wanted to keep teaching; and I needed to stay busy because whenever I didn't have something to do I began to feel sorry for myself. I decided to work with public speaking and writers groups.

As a published writer I felt I could help writers. When my participatory learning manual came out in 1991, I had to go on the road to schools to sell it. It was then that I became comfortable with public speaking. I felt that I could help speakers. I worked many hours with both groups.

In 1997 I began the Word Wits Writers and Speakers Bureau, which is a worldwide nonprofit writers and speakers bureau that provides writer and speaker support services to members while developing specialized programs that suit the individual needs of its clientele. This bureau has kept me busy. Sometimes my husband and I think it takes too much of my time; however, I feel good helping others to succeed, and he is genuinely proud of my success.

My work with The Compassionate Friends is focused on helping other bereaved parents through the most difficult time in their lives.

I changed my focus from me succeeding to helping others succeed.

I have been through other changes since Peter John died.

At first, I couldn't eat. Sure, I thought that I was eating. But I obviously wasn't eating enough. I lost fifteen pounds in the first three months. I guess I just ate a little at every meal; but I just didn't care about food.

When our daughter, Jane, came home from her mission, I began to cook homemade meals for her, my husband, and our parents. I seemed to relax a little when preparing them. It made me feel good to feed others. We all enjoyed it so much; everyone called it "Thanksgiving Dinner" every time I cooked.

Eventually my taste buds heightened again, and the desire to eat returned. Then, I found that I had gained too much weight, and I had to do something about it.

I was going to try to exercise and eat less to lose the weight, but an unfortunate turn of events affected my family and me. Recently, the Vietnamese boy, Quy, who Peter and I had legal custody of since he was in first grade, was killed in a car accident.

Our daughter was extremely helpful. She was a mini-mom to Peter John and Quy. She didn't need a curfew. She always came home at a reasonable hour. She became a Sunday school teacher when she was in college, and after college she became a missionary.

My husband and I tried to bring the boys up right. We moved into the country so they would grow up in a rural atmosphere. They had lots of animals they helped take care of. Both boys became responsible. We made sure they had a Christian foundation. We tried to bring them up honest, with respect for others.

Peter John became an upstanding, confident, and caring adult by the time he turned 18. We were always proud of him. Quy had some problems during his early adult years, most likely due to his situation as a Vietnamese refugee. But, he straightened out and became a helpful, respectful, grateful, thoughtful young man. We will always miss Quy, and are most thankful he became part of our family.

Peter John was going to college, yet he was also building an automobile mechanic business. He died doing what he loved.

I offer this advice for other bereaved parents.

Take care of yourself. Don't expect others to help you. They're uncomfortable with the situation, and they're able to avoid it. Sometimes, some people may be attentive to your needs. Graciously accept whatever help they give. If they ask what you need, tell them. You can make a list of things that need to be done and have it ready to use if anyone should ask. However, if you are the kind of independent person who helps everyone else, others may assume that you can take care of yourself.

Do not make big decisions for about a year. Your mind is not really clear enough. If you have to make a big decision, try to decide on something that can be changed later.

Do what you want to do during holidays. Let your family and friends know how you need to spend the day. They can respect your decision or not. You need to adhere to your plan.

If you need to cry, let it happen. Don't be afraid to let others see you. Crying is a healthy vent for your grief.

Deal with your grief. It is much healthier to plow through it. Research grief. Find a support group. If needed find a grief counselor. Educate those closest to you about grief. That will help them to help you.

I miss Peter John. I remember him as always being helpful, warm, and loving. I could always count on him for support. Peter John was always sweet, not only to me, but to everyone. He listened well. He helped everyone out. He loved life, living and everyone. Peter John was innovative. He always invented whatever he needed. He was an artist. He drew technical things like a camera and almost made it look like a mirror image of the object. He enjoyed writing.

I miss his kind eyes, loving hugs, and the honorable young man that he had become.

The tragedy that we have experienced somehow enables us to establish new and more meaningful priorities, to love and to value the people around us with a renewed sense of appreciation and awareness. If any meaning is to exist in our lives ever again, it will develop as a result of a new found sensitivity, love and compassion for others.

PART IV

Yvonne's Story
Brian Richard Lancaster
October 21, 1966—December 22, 1985
Eighteen Years Later

CHAPTER 10

Longing for her child

My heart was pounding as I slowly pushed the door open and reluctantly entered the well-lit room.

I bit my lip, trying to hold back the tears. My 19-year-old son, Brian, had died in a car accident caused by a drunk driver about six months before. I was overcome with disbelief that such a tragedy had struck my family. The grief of losing my son was overwhelming; there seemed to be no place to put my pain.

I felt as though I myself would die longing for my child, longing for the bittersweet memories of the past, longing for the bright dreams we had planned for his future.

I remember sensing the warm, friendly atmosphere in the room where people where drinking coffee and chatting in small groups. The local chapter of The Compassionate Friends had heard about my loss and sent me information about their support group for bereaved parents.

My feet were unsteady as I made my way into the room, toward the group. I was noticed immediately and was warmly greeted by a woman who hugged me and said, "I know what you're going through." Empathy flowed between us, and my eyes exploded into a river of tears.

I could feel the support from all those around me. I knew the people who were consoling me understood my pain. I tried to steady myself. I couldn't believe that so many other people were suffering like I was. The air felt heavy and the room began to spin. I was taken to a chair and given a cold drink.

As the discussion began, my heart ached for those around me. I began to realize I was not alone in my grief.

These people were feeling the loss of their children too. They were surviving. How were they doing it? I listened to the others. Although the circumstances and the ages of the children were different, the common denominator was the same—pain.

The intensity of knowing your child, your own flesh and blood, has gone before you is like nothing else in life. It's the worst thing that can happen to a person, to a family.

For the first time, I felt as if there was hope for me and my family. That maybe, in some way, I would figure out how to survive as these people had done. I wanted to live again; I wanted to rejoin life again. Above all, I loved my surviving children as much as the son I had lost. They still needed me. I knew I must work through my grief as these people were doing.

This was my first visit to The Compassionate Friends, a self-help organization offering friendship and understanding to bereaved parents.

On Dec. 20, 1985, five days before Christmas, my son Brian was a victim of a drunk driver. Brian was also a victim of his own naiveté, being 19 at the time of the accident. Young people think life will go on and on—I believe Brian put himself in a situation that had dangerous elements to it.

Brian was in the company of a friend who was notorious for bad driving. I always felt that Brian, having been a member of Students Against Drunk Driving, should have known better. We had many talks about these kinds of dangers, so I cannot help thinking that perhaps I wasn't clear enough about these dangers in my talks with him. Feelings of horrible, abject guilt can easily overwhelm my soul, even after 18 years.

Brian was a sophomore at a local junior college. He was due to graduate in May, 1986.

I can remember picturing him in his cap and gown on graduation day. All this and so much more was lost in that fateful moment Brian got into the car with his friend. Brian and the friend were at a Christmas party hosted by one of Brian's classmates.

Brian's friend had graduated the year before. I've often thought that Brian may have looked up to him—he was three years older than Brian, and he wanted to follow in his father's footsteps and become a doctor. Brian may have been impressed with his plans. I'll never know now.

Brian did not drink that night; in fact, Brian never drank. He was an athlete, and very concerned about health and nutrition. He loved the ocean and was a certified scuba diver at 15. He was a runner. He played baseball, football, and he loved to shoot hoops. Brian had a great sense of humor and an easy laugh.

The woman who hosted the party for her classmates was one of the older students who had gone back to school after a long absence. After the party, Brian and his friend were going to meet two girls and go out to eat.

This should have been an ordinary Friday night for a couple of young, good-looking guys who were sociable and fun loving.

His friend was drinking heavily at the party; his blood-alcohol level was over .20. Witnesses later testified that he was drinking straight shots of vodka. However, during the investigation, witnesses said he did not appear to be drunk, that he was even horsing around standing on one leg during a conversation.

My daughter Elizabeth, a criminal justice professional, believes that the driver of that fateful night's accident was accustomed to drinking large amounts of alcohol, but in a social setting he acted sober. It was difficult to tell just how drunk he was. The term is "dead-drunk"—people in this situation seem all right, but once they try to do something that concerns motor control, they immediately fall apart.

Brian's car was out of commission, so I think he took the ride with his friend to meet the girls.

Once they were inside the car, it took his friend less than six minutes to lose control and hit a tree near where the party was being held. Excessive speed, alcohol and slippery roads were all part of the cause of the accident. The driver died instantly, losing his entire face in the steering wheel. Brian hit the left side of his head on the doorframe, causing an explosion inside of his brain.

A doctor at the scene performed CPR on Brian, and "brought him back." He was transported to the University of Massachusetts Medical Center in Worcester, MA.

When receiving the news that the accident had happened, I was utterly shocked, stunned, and hysterical that this had happened to my son. Words cannot express my true state of mind at that time.

I was immediately thrown into emotional turmoil with feelings of tremendous guilt, helplessness, and hopelessness that my child was seriously hurt and I was not there to help him in his time of need.

To this day this is a point of horrible dread and emotional conflict for me. As I write about this now my hands tremble. It's hard to forgive myself.

The vigil for Brian lasted less than 48 hours.

The accident happened at approximately 9 p.m. on Fri., Dec. 20, 1985.

Brian was taken by life-flight to the hospital.

He was placed on life-support.

My husband Tim and I had to let him go.

His brain had died.

There was nothing that could be done.

Nothing.

Brian was declared dead at 2 p.m. on Sun., Dec. 22, 1985.

Brian spent 19 years, two months and one day with us.

We donated his kidneys so others might have a better life.

It was a difficult decision to make at the time of such immense shock and grief. At first when the doctor asked me for an organ donation, only a few short minutes after telling me Brian was brain-dead, I was dazed and confused by the suggestion of organ donation. It was hard to rationalize that my son was gone, and it seemed cruel and heartless for anyone to be asking me a question of this nature. I felt selfish and introspective.

I left the room to search my soul. I knew it was the right decision to make, and yet I had to gather all the strength so I could to say "yes" to the doctor. It came to be a decision I have never regretted. I later found out that a 30-year-old man and a 32-year-old woman had a second chance at life, each getting one of Brian's kidneys.

I never fully realized how important organ donation was until it would hit home—18 years after Brian's death.

Then the cold, wintry days following Brian's death settled in. They were the darkest days of my life.

We chose not to have a wake for Brian, but instead a brief calling period just before his funeral. I chose a sky blue coffin for him—like the color of his eyes.

When it came time to view Brian's body I was shaking and crying. My heart was beating so hard and fast I thought I would either have a heart attack or stroke right on the spot. I touched his face, his hands, and his chest. He was so cold. At that moment in time I was frozen with grim reality: this was my baby, my first born. The void was immediate, the pain immeasurable.

I thought about when Brian was born.

I was so young, a mere child myself.

Preparation: very little.

Naiveté: at it's highest.

Knowing what to do with a crying baby: not at all.

It was a difficult birth. My labor started in the early morning hours. Not knowing what to expect, I was amazed by the level of pain. Something was going wrong. I was put under general anesthesia. When I woke up, it was over. I was groggy. Where was my baby?

There was a nurse in the room. I asked, "Where's my baby?" She answered, "You had a boy. We'll be bringing him in shortly." A few minutes later my mother-in-law entered the room with a grave look on her face acting very uncomfortable.

"Well," she said, shifting her shoulders up and down and making weird motions with her mouth, "It's a boy, he's okay, but there's a problem." My heart pounded in my chest. I was paralyzed with fear for my new baby. No words came out of my mouth. "He has a cleft lip. It's not too bad," she said, trying to reassure me. "It's less than an eighth of an inch. There's no palate involvement, thank God. It can be repaired when he's 10 weeks old." I begged, "Bring me my child, my son, please."

Shortly afterward the nurse brought my precious son Brian to me. I took him in my arms and said, "Oh, he's so beautiful, sleeping soundly, my little angel."

His hair was blond, and he had lots of it. His cheeks were full and rosy. As long as I live, I will never, ever, forget one of the three most important moments in my life, the birth of my first angel.

At ten weeks old Brian's lip was repaired by one of the best plastic surgeons on the East Coast. He was left with a tiny pink zigzag scar barely noticeable. He would later grow a moustache in high school. He was absolutely adorable.

And now it had come down to this. A child is not supposed to die before his parents. It's out of the natural order of things.

The funeral was Christmas Eve day. Hundreds of people came to show their love and respect for Brian. Since the ground was covered with snow and frozen, his casket had to be placed in a vault until spring, at which time, he would be buried.

My life fell into a tailspin of grief and emotional turmoil. I didn't know how I could survive. I was a mother whose son had died. How could I possibly live another day?

To make matters even more difficult, my marriage was in trouble, and unfortunately did not survive. We divorced four years after Brian's tragedy...(Today, Tim and I have a genuine, mutual respect for one another, and share equally in the lives of our surviving children, Elizabeth and Timothy, who together, we so dearly love.)

During this early grieving process, nothing seemed rational or reasonable to me. I was often beyond consolation. Our two surviving children, Elizabeth and Timothy, were in their early teens at the time of their brother's death.

It would take the passage of time to help us—to have some new experiences and put distance between Brian's death and us.

I couldn't think, speak, or do much of anything. I worried constantly about my surviving children, and didn't want them out of my sight. We were all hurting so much. We took turns helping each other.

All our days were dark during that first year; there were no good days. We were barely going through the motions of life—showering, school, and work. Both Elizabeth, 15, and Timothy, 14, were so sad. It was a period of time that the world felt like it was standing still. How were we going to survive this? One minute Brian was with us, the next minute he wasn't.

I don't know how Elizabeth and Timothy managed to go back to school, but they did. It wasn't easy for them. I'm sure it was pure torture. I compare that with trying to work again. I felt like people were talking about me, pointing me out, saying, "There's that woman whose son died." I felt people were treating me like a freak.

Trying to regain some kind of normalcy in life after losing a child was a profound struggle.

To survive, I needed to become grounded within family, society and ourselves. The most difficult thing was facing life without Brian. Where did he go? Could I possibly find him somewhere out there? It was a nightmare. Pulling together some coping mechanisms through those dark days was nearly impossible.

With the passage of time came the first round of birthdays, various holidays and family gatherings. These were cold days and dark nights without Brian.

This was so depressing. I remember looking out at the tall pine trees behind my house. I would stare at them for hours at a time, looking upward, looking at the sky, wondering, and waiting. I counted each and every hour of every day that passed, minute by minute.

It was so easy to fall into a total heap crying, shaking, and totally frustrated knowing that I would never see my child again. What in God's name had happened?

I found myself becoming extremely quiet. I never raised my voice, and lost confidence in myself and in the life I used to know. I knew it would be a tough journey. I had a long way to go.

I often had Masses said for Brian trying to keep him alive in a spiritual way and in a way where I thought no one could possibly forget him. We encouraged donations to be made to the National Head Injury Foundation. I established a scholarship fund in Brian's name, hoping his memory would inspire others to achieve.

The first three weeks after Brian's death were filled with writing thank you notes, filling out and filing insurance claims, and notifying the proper parties of Brian's passing. These are things no parent should ever have to do for a child.

The first three years after Brian died were extremely difficult. The first year was the worst.

My weight dropped considerably. I couldn't sleep or think straight. Even though I had always been a person of faith, it was shaken to the core. I was so angry with God, the drunk driver, and with myself for having survived my child. The physical and psychological pain brought me to my knees. Brian's death humbled me to the very heart of my soul.

I had a candle burning for Brian, every day and every night. I placed one at the cemetery that would burn for a week at a time.

CHAPTER 11

In dreams he comes

There was never a day I didn't go the cemetery and kneel at Brian's gravesite. Tears would stream down my face as I prayed. I would leave little gifts, notes, and flowers. I would always hug the small gravestone before I left. Sometimes I would just sit in the car and cry. I didn't know what else to do; I felt it was the only thing I could do—I missed him so much.

I regretted burying him. I would often imagine that I could dig him up and take him home, one way or another, no matter what.

There were many times during the first year or so that I know my thinking was irrational.

There was a particular young man at the grocery store that looked very much like Brian. He always smiled and said hello to me, and I always reciprocated. We got to know each other, and talked. He was an only child, the same age as Brian. We would chat lightly, and always wish each other a good day. I felt it was a small gift from heaven, to have him to chat with and look at from time to time. I would fantasize that he was "up for adoption" and would come and live with us. I told Elizabeth about him. She agreed he was a Brian look-a-like. For all of the time he worked in the grocery store, we exchanged pleasantries and wishes for a good day.

During many sleepless nights I made many calls to my family and close friends to talk. Their love and patience helped to stabilize and ground me, but it wasn't enough. I went to my family doctor, and he prescribed a tranquilizer and antidepressant. The tranquilizer helped me sleep and cope with the pain. I had some relief. The antidepressant helped to stabilize my emotional state, and I wasn't crying every second of every day. This helped me both physically and emotionally. It was the right thing for me to do. I was able to get my bearings some of the time. This therapy helped me to help my surviving children. I was able to cope better during my waking hours.

Before Brian's accident, I worked as a writer, photographer, and public speaker. I loved what I was doing. I was often in the pubic eye due to publication of my weekly newspaper column and profiles of local people. My need for privacy and anonymity during this period of time meant that I had to leave my public persona behind.

I continued to write my weekly column because I could do that in the privacy of my home and submit my work without seeing too many people. The profiles became very difficult. I had to face people and that made me uncomfortable. Many people knew me in the community, and would either broach the subject of Brian, or "interview" me about my life. Or sometimes there was something in their lives that would spontaneously trigger my grief. It was too painful to handle.

I modified my line of work to stay afloat during the first year of my grief. I took a temporary job as an administrative assistant in another city. No one knew me or knew my background. I was anonymous.

I gained a measure of peace this way, allowing me a certain amount of personal space and a reclusive period in my life in order to cope with my loss of Brian. I needed time…

Dreams have a way of helping; dreams have a way of hurting; dreams have the ability to make you feel even lonelier than before the dream began or ended. Sometimes dreams are appreciated. It can be a tough call when you're dealing with the loss of your child.

I wasn't fully awake, but drifting and in out. Peeking slightly out of one eye told me the sun was beginning to filter through the window. I was feeling drowsy and bathed in the soft colors of my room.

Something, someone, touched my big toe and began to wiggle it back and forth. With a start, I sat up straight wondering who was in my room. Clutching the blankets, I looked toward the end of the bed. There was no one there. I thought one of the kids had silently crept in and decided to play a game with me.

Looking under the bed the only thing I could see was dust. The sun came streaming through as the cold winter morning seemed to beckon me to my feet.

Who touched my toe? It was very real, I thought, scratching my head. My senses were coming to, as I stepped into my slippers.

"Why," I thought, "it was Brian!"

It was clearly something he would have done—the prankster, the big mom teaser. He wiggled my toe. He had paid me a visit.

Clouds surrounded my feet and swirled in a whirlwind all around me, like a rock concert where the performers disappear in a cloud of smoky magic. Not being able to see clearly, I waited patiently until my vision cleared.

Off in the distance was a hospital bed bathing my son in soft white lights. My heart jumped. I began to run, my legs and arms heavy. I moved in slow motion toward my son. Without speaking, he turned his face to me, and a peaceful smile appeared.

"Brian," I gasped, "where have you been? I've been looking all over for you?"

We were now both bathed in the soft white light from above the bed. "Mom, I'm all right. I'm okay," he said softly.

With a flash, he was gone, the white light disappeared, and the clouds were swept away. I stood alone sobbing, unable to comprehend why he couldn't stay. Emptiness filled my heart and soul.

It was a fitful sleep, tossing and turning. Somewhere between the Alpha and Beta zones, Brian popped into my mind and was scurrying all over the place.

He appeared to be about three years old: tousled blond hair, striped short sleeve shirt, shorts, and little boots, and impossible to catch. He was running and hiding behind everything, trees, houses, furniture. I just couldn't catch him. I shouted, "Brian, where have you been? Come here. Come see mommy!" He giggled and ran. I felt totally frustrated trying to catch him, trying to make him listen. "Everyone wants to know where you have been? Please come to mommy!"

I managed to get a little closer to him. We held hands. His hand was very little in mine. "I've been here all the time, Mom," he said. "No you haven't. I've been looking all over for you. I miss you so much," I said, my voice being caught up in the restless night...

The clouds swirled.

The football field was barren. There were two women sitting in low chairs, chatting. Seeing Brian in the distance, I moved away from them, running toward my boy. My heart pounded as we ran toward each other, meeting in a long overdue embrace. Feeling happy and sad at the same time, we hugged knowing this would be a brief encounter; we made the most of it.

Proud and excited, I brought him over to the two women sitting in low chairs. I stammered, not remembering their names. It didn't matter. I was three feet off of the ground. "This is my son Brian," I said, more of a declaration than an introduction.

Walking together, arm in arm, I asked him, "Have you had a chance to give anyone the tour of our old neighborhood?" Looking off in the distance, he nodded his head with a simple, "Yes."

With that, he disappeared into the vastness of the field.

This is how my dream ended and my day began.

It's always nice to see Brian, if only in my dreams. Yes, it was a visit from Brian, desolate from my perspective. In dreams at least I get to see him, to talk with him if ever so briefly.

Through the years, I've come to realize that parents who have lost their children manage to cope and survive in many different ways. Some people don't survive very well. Some don't survive at all.

I met John through The Compassionate Friends. John died from a broken heart. He only lived about 3 years after his son, Stephen, was killed in a motorcycle accident. John was quiet, reserved, and during The Compassionate Friends meetings he would express the loss of his son eloquently while holding back his tears and trying to help others who were newly bereaved.

When I was in high school I met a lady named Rose. Her teenage son, Jimmy, died from leukemia. All she did was smoke cigarettes and cry. She worked nights so she didn't have to sleep. Rose did not live long after Jimmy's death; there was no consoling her. She was obsessed with Jimmy. Nothing else mattered. She used to keep a high school graduation picture of Jimmy on her kitchen counter where she would stand and smoke while recalling stories of her Jimmy. I clearly remember thinking of how tragic this loss was, and knew Rose was not long for this world either.

Little did I know at the time that I, too, would lose my son some day.

Grief is heavy, all consuming, powerful, and often insidious. Without a word of warning it can make your heart pound, confuse your thinking, and drag you kicking and screaming into the depths of despair. At times my longing for my lost child has been so potent for me that I thought, like John and Rose; I would surely die of a broken heart.

In my life I have found people to be, generally speaking, optimistic and understanding.

We have all seen people rise from the ashes and conquer fear, pain, and personal losses of unimaginable magnitude. Through grief I've changed in ways that I never expected. It deepened my sense of compassion for others who were going through difficult times.

There are no ways to prepare for a tragedy. In fact, it would be downright morbid to even think about it.

In the work place I helped everyone I could by lending an ear and offering encouragement that things will get better, while assuring them that the dawn always comes again. I developed more patient ways; and the usual small inconveniences of daily life, such as a flat tire or a long line at the super market, became inconsequential.

I'm afraid the things I miss most about my son would fill a book. It's easy for me to say I miss the sound of his voice, his laugh, and watching him move about, bantering with his brother and sister. I miss hearing the three of them debate the hot topics of the day, going at it with three different opinions and with such intensity that sometimes I felt more like a referee than their mother.

99

I miss Brian's tales of the sea. He would always bring home seashells, sand dollars, and talk about how truly peaceful it was under the ocean. He was funny. He let Elizabeth and Timothy try on his diving gear, and then took pictures of them.

Brian was also the ultimate teaser, especially with his sister.

It's funny thinking back on how precious those days were, how very innocent and wonderful they were.

I would race my children. The four of us would line up. Ready. On your mark. Get set. Go! For a long time I could beat them, but when Brian was about 12 he beat me, soundly. He was way ahead of me laughing his head off. We also ran a town-sponsored five-mile race. Brian was way out there with the top runners. Elizabeth ran with her friends and did just great. I don't recall Timothy running, but I do remember one little kid who ran home instead of running the race. It was great fun. I miss those days.

Brian had a girlfriend at the time of his death. She grieved heavily for him. There wasn't much I could do to console her; I was inconsolable myself. I never saw her again after the funeral.

The first three years after Brian's death were the most difficult. I liken it to rising from the ashes, a little at a time. Most of the time I felt emotionally and spiritually spent, heartsick.

Brian's death humbled me to where I found that I had to begin again with regard to faith, hope and a renewal of courage in order to carry on. It was difficult, if not impossible, to rationalize that I would pull through this with my mind intact and with my family whole.

After work I often went to bed, or stared at the television sipping a glass of wine. I slept. I dragged myself through most days. I would smile and talk with my surviving children and do as many things with and for them that I could possibly do.

Along with my immediate family, my children were the beacons shining from the lighthouse beside Brian's ocean of love. Their light shone through the darkest of days and the loneliest of nights. I knew we all had a long way to go. I wanted to get there together. Deep down inside I didn't want to give up. That's not my nature. I've always been a fighter.

During the first three years following Brian's death I took my time doing things and spent much of it alone.

I gradually began to eat again and occasionally attended a family function for a brief period. I gave Brian's belongings to Elizabeth and Timothy. I still have one of his jackets hanging in the closet, and his bathrobe is still not very far away.

Being able to get through a day without crumbling emotionally was one of the indicators that I would survive; and if I could survive, then the children would too.

I came to my own conclusion that physical separation is a very important aspect of grieving.

We're human beings. It's the element of acceptance that takes time, and it's impossible to say just how long that will take. We're all individuals. The way it felt for me was akin to learning how to use an arm or a leg again after being paralyzed or having a limb amputated. Step by step, little by little.

The spiritual and emotional acceptance for me was much different than the physical acceptance. In my heart of hearts, and through my life-long religious beliefs, I felt that Brian was experiencing a new life with God in heaven. My mother's prayer and wish has always been that he is in a better, higher place where there is no suffering or anxiety.

I believe that we will be reunited one day, that we will hug and kiss each other that together we will bask in God's eternal love.

The physical and emotional separation is a difficult road. I have come to feel an innate sense of serenity and dignified acceptance of what happened.

As a family we light candles in Brian's memory and speak lovingly and fondly of his life and legacy. It doesn't need to be his birthday, or Christmas, or any other special day. Every day is special because of having had Brian in our lives, and knowing he is watching out for us from Heaven above.

I see Brian in his brother and sister, his cousins, aunts, uncles, nieces and nephews.

Brian is the gentle rain drops on the window pane. He's the bloom of springtime flowers. He's every wave that washes ashore, and every star that shines in Heaven. He's the moon's glow, the autumn breeze and every ray of sunlight through my kitchen window. He's in the dawn, daylight, dusk, in the gloaming as the sun sets, and in the cool night air that taps me on the cheek.

On my dark days I thought of Brian's spirit and a light would shine through my heart and soul.

I have so very much to look forward to in spite of my grief.

Rebuilding a family, a life, took time. Some of the turning points came slowly, but they came. Elizabeth graduated from college and went on to get a master's degree in criminal justice. Timothy graduated from college with a degree in music. This year Tim received his medical degree, and is currently an emergency room doctor. Ten years after Brian's death, I remarried a wonderful man, Neil, who is kind and caring. With his two children, Evan and Gwenythe, I have two more. Together, we have eight grandchildren. Also, Neil bought me a miniature poodle we named Minnie Mae. She, too, is a bright spot for me, and a wonderful addition to our family. Minnie can restore flagging spirits on any given day. She is always there, a fine pet indeed.

Still, Brian is gone. There will always be a missing piece of my heart.

He was a wonderful young man who I'm proud to say was my son for 19 years. Some days I stare at his writing, at the last note he wrote to me. "Dear Mom—I stopped by to say hi. Sorry I missed you. Will call you later. Love, Bri."

There would never be a later.

I'm sorry I missed you too, Brian.

CHAPTER 12

Coming full circle

The telephone rang Oct. 17, 2004, at 1:10 a.m.

My husband Neil jumped up. He picked up the phone after the next short, piercing ring.

I never moved a muscle. I lay there holding my breath wondering what this late-night phone call was all about.

"Yes," Neil answered as he swung his legs over the side of the bed, "this is he." Then, after a pause, he said, "Yes, I'm ready to go forward." He snapped on the night-table lamp and squinted at the clock. "We can be there in about an hour. Thank you." He hung up.

I was afraid to ask.

"That was the transplant center," Neil said. "We need to leave for the hospital right away," he said pulling on sweat pants. "They have a kidney for me. They said it's a perfect match."

I remained silent and unmoving. I was in shock.

During the previous two years Neil had been in the final stages of renal failure due to diabetes. He had suffered greatly from complications: headaches, vomiting, diarrhea, exhaustion, bloating. He was seeing a nephrologist and many other physicians who were preparing him for impending dialysis. Stoic throughout, Neil never complained. He always kept a positive attitude and felt luckier than most.

Neil's sister, Kathleen, his son, Evan, and my daughter, Elizabeth, were all willing to donate one of their kidneys to Neil. His sister was the best match, five out of six panels. Six is considered a perfect match and reduces the chances of rejection. If Neil had received a kidney from Evan, a 50-50 match, the chances for rejection would have been higher. In Elizabeth's case, she could not donate to Neil directly; her blood type did not match his. Elizabeth and Neil's kidney transplant situation would have been what is called a cross donation, which would have involved two other participants, making the set of circumstances much more complicated.

It is not easy to ask for, nor is it easy to accept an offer for a kidney from a willing family member or a friend. It made us feel uncomfortable, but we had been reassured by health care professionals that a healthy person can live a normal life with one functioning kidney. Also, there was never a doubt in anyone's mind that Neil would do it for them if the situations were reversed.

Often people would ask me, "Is Neil on a list for a kidney?"

My response was always the same. "No, Neil is not on a list for a kidney. He has to be on dialysis before he can be on the list."

Standard procedure for patients in renal failure is to get a blood test once a month which is sent to a repository for special screening. The chances that Neil would receive a kidney through this method before actually being placed on the list were remote. To get a kidney at this stage would mean that the kidney would have to be a perfect match—six out of six panels.

I kept wondering why Neil got this phone call as we drove to the hospital.

We arrived at the hospital just after 2 a.m. Neil approached the emergency room desk. "I'm here to get a kidney transplant," he said.

"We've been waiting for you," one of the women said.

A nurse got up and took us to a room off to the side.

"They told me this kidney is a perfect match for you." She looked at us. "I told them there is no such thing as a perfect match, but they told me this was a perfect match. It's like you won the lottery or got struck by lightening," she said. "The odds are astronomical."

My heart flooded with memories of Brian's tragedy and loss.

"We're so sad for the donor family. Someone is grieving right now," I said, remembering and knowing what that devastation is all about. Tears rolled down my cheeks.

"That's true," the nurse said, "but it was their decision to donate their son's kidneys. It's a gift for your husband."

Neil and I were ushered into a special area in the emergency room. Many hospital personnel came through explaining the transplant surgery and telling us what to expect. The surgery would be performed once all of the members of the transplant team arrived at about 7:30 a.m.

I made some telephone calls to our children and other family members.

While waiting in the emergency room, we huddled together on a gurney and fell asleep in each other's arms. All too soon they came and rolled Neil away to the operating room. So many unexpected things happened during that October night; it was overwhelming and miraculous all at the same time. The operation took much of the day.

Neil was successfully transplanted. Now, four months into his recovery, there have been no signs of rejection and he is doing very well.

When Neil awoke from the surgery he looked at me and whispered, "Brian—it's a miracle from Brian."

Due to confidentiality, we will never know the donor's name or the circumstances of his death, but we do know the donor was a 26-year-old man who had been in an accident and that his mother was the one who gave permission to donate his kidneys.

Since the New England Organ Bank encourages letters of thanks to the donor family, I took the first opportunity to write a letter while Neil was still recovering in the hospital. In addition to expressing deep gratitude to the donor family, I also told them about Brian and that I, too, had lost a child and donated his kidneys. I hope that in some small way this may have comforted the donor family to know that the gift of life had come full circle.

We often light candles and pray for the donor and his family. We will forever cherish their unselfish decision.

As I look out of the window on this cold February day, I imagine myself as a little girl, swinging in a warm summer sunset, pigtails flying high, waiting for my father to come home. Yes, of course, life was very simple then. As children we are innocent, not worried about tomorrow, and we live for the moment. Naturally, we are unknowing about what the future may hold; and unfamiliar territories are charted with words like challenge, courage and bravery. During childhood, there are no reference points for these words.

Life indeed has had some knocked-out, dragged-out battles along the way. And, for me, I have learned many lessons about patience, listening, and appreciating each day of my life with those I love and care about. I take nothing for granted. I'm glad I'm still in it, boxing gloves and all.

As the little girl on the swing, I never dreamed I would one day lose one of my own precious children. As the little girl on the swing, I never would have guessed my husband would have to fight for his life.

There is no preparing for some of life's events. We can only hope that by sharing love, compassion and lessons learned along the way, we can help one another get through life's darkest moments.

PART V

The Four Mothers in Conversation

CHAPTER 13

Reaching out to other bereaved parents

Anne, Jane, Deb and Yvonne had many meetings during the year and a half it took them to write *Every Step of the Way*. Through their many discussions they journeyed together as a small band of mothers who wanted to give meaning to their sons' lives, and to give hope to other bereaved parents by sharing their passage through grief and beyond. This is one of their heart-to-heart conversations.

Worrying about our children

Yvonne: When we talk like this, I realize we have so many similarities. Just talking about Sunday's service (Compassionate Friends annual candle lighting service in December) and they start to show photos of the kids, its like how did we get here? It seemed like it was all boys, young men. You know, like an epidemic of accidents, things that went wrong. It seemed like they were all young men. There was a real trend there, I have to say. I know people have lost daughters, but boy, where have all the young men gone? I had to wonder about that. It's a certain part of life, I think, for young people. You do worry. You have the right to worry. It's frightening. I said to myself, "Gee, didn't I tell Brian often enough about the things about life? Did I miss something?"

Anne: I ask myself that all the time. My son used to always say, "Don't worry, Mom." He said that to me. When I think about it now, I did worry, and I should have been worried. I had a reason to worry. He tried to tell me not to worry.

Deb: I always told him, "I love you! Be safe!" and gave him a hug and a little kiss on the cheek when he was leaving. Somehow I thought that would protect him. That morning I did nothing differently. But I never saw him safe and sound again. After his death, I constantly thought of things that I could have done differently…things that I could have done to keep him safe. Mothers are supposed to keep their children safe. But, I failed to keep my son safe.

Jane: But it's also something we don't have control over. I mean, I used to worry about Chris. He traveled so much. I always had this thing where I said, "Call me when you get there. Call me when you get in." And he did. He would call me, and when he didn't I would call and say, "I know your plane landed because I checked with the airport. Why didn't you call me?" He was walking home in his neighborhood. How is there anything that you could or could not have done? How is there anything that you could have foreseen? There isn't. It's just what I think was meant to be, however awful that sounds. I just don't think that there is an answer.

Yvonne: I know, I don't think there is either. Boy, did I search for one, too.

Jane: I did, too. I still do. When I think of that night that Chris was murdered, he was walking home from this restaurant. Well, it was late. I know he had beers when he went there. He was watching the game, and he was talking to the people there. He used to socialize over there all the time. He could have driven. If he'd had his car, he probably would be alive today; but he didn't drive. He just was being responsible. And while he was being responsible, he got murdered. So I mean there is no answer. It isn't because he was not driving. It's just that there is no answer. There is no answer.

Yvonne: There really isn't. And I think it's ridiculous to say that someone was in the wrong place at the wrong time. It's stupid! It's such a cliché. And when you really think about it, it's like that makes no sense at all.

Jane: I know. What is really offensive about it is that it puts the blame on them. It's like saying they are to blame for being dead; like it's their fault, if they weren't there they wouldn't be dead. I think where I get angry is that nobody seems to say that about a criminal. They don't ask, "Why were they there?" Then you get into the act of them getting into prison, and you get all the criminals' rights and things that come up. The thing is when a person is dead, it's almost like people want to find every reason why they should not be dead; and that means that the person did something wrong. Even if it isn't a murder, even if it's an accident, the first thing they look at is: what did they do? Many times it may be something they did. Other times it's something somebody else did. But there's just the almost natural need to insulate yourself so that you can say to yourself, "Well this wouldn't happen to me because I wouldn't be there."

Yvonne: I agree with you. It's like with our boys (Yvonne's, Deb's, and Anne's); they weren't in the wrong place. It's ridiculous to think that because people are living their lives whether it's good, bad, or indifferent. It's life. So it's not something we should feel guilty about, but it's hard not to sometimes. You survive.

Jane: Survivor's guilt, I guess.

Christmas time

Yvonne: Brian died right at Christmas time. We buried him Christmas Eve. This is the very first year we've had lights outside. It was really like a nightmare, 17 years.

Jane: I feel less guilty because I don't do anything. I don't do anything.

Yvonne: And that's okay. It has been seventeen years. This is the first time we've put up a tree. Our daughter is going to help us.

Anne: Really? It was the first time you've had a tree? Wow!

Yvonne: Seventeen years, it's been a long time. Little trees, table tops. It's kind of amazing, really. Mostly for the kids.

Anne: So, it's still a painful time for you?

Yvonne: It really is because people look at Christmas as a happy time. It's the time I buried my child. How can that be happy? Even though the rest of us always feel happy, this isn't a happy time for us.

It's really difficult for the surviving kids because they grieve. They can't celebrate easily. How can they? Their brother died. I think this will be good for our daughter, too. She's going to come over tomorrow. I think that will be good.

Jane: Did you keep the decorations that you had?

Yvonne: Yes. I'll use them this year.

Jane: I don't know that I could ever use them. The thing is the last Christmas that we had together; I really decorated the house. It was my first year of not working, my first year retired. I was all gung-ho about not having to work. So I put a lot of time into decorating. The kids were all coming home for Christmas, so it was fun to do. When I think of it, that's what I remember, enjoying decorating. Nobody was going to be in the house but the kids when they came home. Then I put those decorations away after Christmas, and I've never taken them out again. I said to Amy, "I don't want anything to do with those decorations." I said, "I don't know what you guys want to do." She said, "Well, I want them." I said, "Okay, that's all I need to know." That's fine. Their stockings are in there.

Yvonne: I didn't have anything in there like that, but I think if I did I wouldn't be able to use it.

Jane: What Amy did a couple of years ago she bought us new stockings. She got kind of like funny ones, the Cat In The Hat kind of thing which was very, very different from what we had, and she hangs them at her house. That's where we have Christmas.

Deb: I know that I've been very quiet. Peter John died in September. I guess that makes us lucky because we don't associate his death with Christmas. The first Christmas, we couldn't even think about decorating. But then our daughter was coming home for a week from her mission. She was a missionary in Washington State, so we did not get to see her too often. As a result, we mustered a small tree, a few very basic decorations, and a couple of gifts for her under the tree. We all had stockings: the three children, my mother and father, my husband's mother, my husband and I, and small ones for each of the animals. Those stockings have never come out of storage since Peter John's death. I can't bear to look at them. We bought Jane a fancy new stocking that first year. In the years since then, we put up more and more decorations until we have surpassed what we used to put up. However, the decorations that we put up now are not childish, but are much more sophisticated.

The day the earth stood still

Yvonne: When you found out; you're never going to forget that. It's a moment frozen in time, and you are never, ever, ever going to be the same.

Jane: Yes, there was life before that moment, and there is life after. I remember being aware of that standing in that hall. I remember knowing our life is over. What I meant was the life that we knew. I remember knowing at that moment that life never ever ever was going to be the same again. There was a life, and now would be another.

Deb: At the moment that I held my son's lifeless body, I knew that nothing would ever be the same. It couldn't be. Peter John would not physically be with us anymore. The happy family that I knew would be tormented by the grief, need to work really hard on rebuilding their lives, and would never be that happy again.

Anne: I don't think I knew that then because I was so shocked and numbed by the news that I didn't even cry. I was just so, my brain went into an immediate state of shock. But I sure knew it afterwards. And the way I thought of it is, I don't know if you remember there was a movie called "The Day the Earth Stood Still." At the time the movie was popular I was nine or ten years old, but I remember the name of that movie. I remember the concept of the earth standing still, how intriguing is that? After Michael died, that (movie) came back to me and I thought, this is a perfect description of what has happened to me. The earth stood still in my life on May 15, 2001. It's never going to be the same, as you say.

Writing about grief

Deb: Basically, I have written a couple of articles, a few speeches for bereavement seminars, and a short story. Occasionally, I've even been inspired to write a poem. As the leader of The Compassionate Friends, I do counsel people to write about their feelings in a journal, as it seems to help them work through their grief.

Yvonne: I just type it out (writing about grief).

Jane: I do what you do. I have to sort of type it out when it hits me. The other night I stayed up until 3:30 in the morning writing. It's funny that sometimes at 1 or 2 a.m. your best thoughts come out. I was able to put down everything I was thinking about. Sometimes I think it's Chris, too. I remember when I wrote my impact statement. I would write it, and rewrite it, and rewrite it. I gave it to my grief therapist to read. She loved it. She thought that I had really expressed myself well. She said, "Jane, just be yourself and let what you feel come out." I'm reading over it in bed one day, it was almost like Chris was looking over my left shoulder.

All of a sudden I looked at it, and I said, "I left the most important part out of this."

What I had left out was how devastating it was for me to know that he had died alone on that street and was there for hours. Especially where I was a nurse, and I used to spend my time with hospice patients and hold their hands, and my son died alone. It was so weird to read this whole thing that I thought was absolutely perfect, and I looked at it and said, "I left out the most important thing." I almost started to laugh because I said, "Chris, you're making me write it out!" It was almost like I could feel him right over my shoulders saying, "Well it's all right, but you forgot this," because that's exactly what I forgot. Two years later when I went to see George Anderson, that's the part he brought out—how obsessed I was over how Chris had died. So I rewrote it. It was almost like Chris was right there directing me. You know, you can just be looking at it and all of a sudden something will just hit you. I brought it back to my grief therapist and said, "I left something out and then I remembered." She read it, and she said, "This is perfect now." It just felt so good.

114

The judge asked me if he could have a copy.

Yvonne: Wow, that's powerful.

Deb: You did a great job! Chris must be very proud of his mom!

Jane: Chris was going to have the last word at that arraignment. That was how I felt. I didn't even ask them if they allowed an impact statement. I said I was going to be giving it. I just told my victim's advocate that I want to give an impact statement, and so they let me.

Yvonne: They guide us though, don't they? They guide us if we let them.

Anne: The other night after writing did you go to sleep?

Jane: Yes, I did.

Anne: Did you dream about anything after you had been writing?

Jane: No, I don't think so. I don't think I did. I just felt good. All of a sudden it was just like, I just let it all hang out. Maybe I needed to have it be 3:30 in the morning. I don't know.

Yvonne: It's almost like enlightenment, isn't it?

Jane: Yes, it is.

Anne: For me it's still there. It's so new. I'm still obsessed with him everyday, all day. I'm still at that point, so for me to have a way to release that and to express it is very therapeutic.

Yvonne: I'm finding that it is, too. And I'm thinking to myself that the most therapeutic thing is to think that it could help someone else.

Contacts and friendships

Jane: You're really in a different world. It's a different world once this happens.

The friendships are different. Even the ones that stay, they change. Life is just very, very different.

Yvonne: I couldn't even go back to the same town. I had a hard time working. I had to change that because I thought people were looking at me. And I kept thinking in my mind this really didn't happen, you know, he's still alive. That was tough.

Anne: I feel that now. It's hard to go into the grocery store and see people who live in my hometown. You know that the instant they see you they are thinking, you know, her son died.

Deb: I found it really hard to go to my grocery store. You see, my son worked there part time and he used to bring his grandmother there to do her shopping once a week. The manager was one of the pallbearers. They all knew me. But sometimes they were easier to face then neighbors and old friends who were genuinely stumped at what to say to me. They didn't have to avoid me at times because sometimes I avoided them. I could not face helping them to deal with my grief and me.

Yvonne: I remember one time when I went to the post office, this was during the first year, and I used to dread it. A lady came up to me and said, "So how are you doing? People are saying you are disturbed." Disturbed? I was mortified. I wasn't the same person. I wasn't on the school committee anymore. I wasn't, you know, the bouncing writer anymore.

Anne: You are disturbed. Something very disturbing happened in your life.

Yvonne: You know, like I was a mental case. Here I was still working and trying to maintain a home and somebody said that I was disturbed. People were talking about me. You get to feel that you want to be, you know, you don't want anyone to talk to you.

Jane: I got so bad; I wouldn't even go to the store. I used to ask people to do that for me. I really felt agoraphobic, I really did. I didn't want to answer the phone.

Yvonne: I also didn't go to any weddings or anything, nothing for a long, long time. I just really started to do things again. That's, I guess, a breakthrough in some way. I couldn't stand to see any young man dance with his mother.

Jane: I know, I usually leave the room at that time. That's the last time Chris was home, it was for Amy's wedding. When he danced with me, he said, "I love you, Mom." I'll never forget that.

Yvonne: What fine sons we had, though. And we really loved them. We did.

Looking for our children in public places

Yvonne (speaking about the boy at Victory Market who looked like Brian): There was such suffering. He looked just like Brian, just like him! You know the thick blond hair. He always talked to me. He was the same age.

Anne: I'm always looking for Michael, maybe because it's still so new. My daughter and I went out to a restaurant a few weeks ago. There was a kid who was about his age who was sitting a couple of tables away from us. I focused on his hands. Throughout the entire meal, I looked at that boy's hands. He was the same size as Michael. His hands reminded me of Michael. It was very difficult for me not to go over to him and ask if I could hold his hand.

Deb: We see their body type, hairstyle, or a facial likeness and we want to look more and even hold that moment in time forever. If we could get a photo of it, we'd be happy, at least for a moment.

Jane: Last year my aunt died. Her grandson from California came, and I had not seen him in like ten or fifteen years. He is a young man now. I looked at him, and he was the picture of Chris. Everybody noticed it. The hair coloring. He had a mustache like Chris. He had the same sort of body build, and I kept looking at him. Finally, I said to him, "My God, you look just like Chris!" He said, "You know, everybody's been telling me that." So finally, I started laughing and sort of made a joke out of it. His cousin was getting married the next year, and I said, "Please tell me you are coming to this wedding so that I can just sit and look at you." When he was leaving, I said, "I have to give you a hug." It felt like I was hugging Chris. It just was the nicest thing.

Yvonne: This sounds so familiar. I thought I was the only one who did that. We all do it.

Anne: I wonder when you stop doing it.

Deb: When we brought our daughter to Disney World to help her begin to live again, she saw a manikin that she thought looked so much like her bother that she made us go on the World ride again to see him.

117

Yvonne: I have a great nephew who looks a lot like Brian. But he's got long hair. You know, I just want to fix him up so he looks exactly like him. It wouldn't take much. I'd have to change the way his hair is cut. It's just how you feel. It's just how you feel. You want to do that.

Yvonne: It's the contact. That's why that dream was so special. When I woke up, I wanted to fall back to sleep again.

Anne: What was the dream about?

Yvonne: We were sitting and talking. But I can't remember what we talked about.

The message I got was that he was okay. That's how I felt. It was so real. It's only in my dream, but I'll take it. But it's not good enough. It's really not.

Jane: I know, it's great for the moment. Then you want it back again.

You will survive

Jane: That is really what you need to hear. That is what you really need to know.

I was obsessed with that. My brother was dating this girl that lost a child. She had lost a child when he was three years old. The night that Chris was murdered, she was the only person I wanted to talk to. I hardly knew her. I needed to hear from her that I was going to survive this night, never mind next week. It wasn't her, it was her experience. I remember wanting to speak with (a woman at my church who had lost a child), but she was out of town. The need to touch base with somebody who had survived it was the most compelling feeling that I ever had. The only way I can equate it is I think I must have felt like an alcoholic feels when they really need that drink. I needed to know somebody who was going to be able to tell me something.

Anne: I thought of Jane the first day that Michael died. I believe that sometimes things happen in life for a reason. When I was 15 years old, my best friend was a cousin of Jane's husband. My friend and I babysat for Ray and Jane. Chris was a toddler, and we babysat him and (Chris' siblings) the twins. The Maki's moved away, so I hadn't seen Chris since he was seven or eight years old. When I married, I moved to the same town. My husband was the one who saw the article in the newspaper about Chris' murder. We went to the wake. I remember commenting to my husband that Ray and Jane were still standing and talking to people, that they didn't die. I frequently thought of Chris over the three or four years after he died and before my son died. I thought about their family and prayed for them. Then when Michael died, the Maki's came to my mind. I drew strength from remembering Jane at the funeral home when Chris had died. When we had the wake and funeral for my son, I believe part of the reason I was able to stand and breathe and hug people was because I remembered she had done it. Jane and Ray came to Michael's funeral. The friend whom I'd known as a teenager is no longer part of my life, that relationship went away. I see things in a spiritual way. I believe it was known on a spiritual level that I would need this person (Jane) later in my life.

Jane: I agree.

Deb: I guess that my husband and I never made a choice about surviving because we had several elderly people that needed us to be strong so that we could continue to take care of them. Thinking about it now, I guess we knew that we would have to make it and we have.

Friends who cannot attend funeral services

Jane: I understand when people can't come to the funeral because they can't handle it, but if they've been that involved in your life they should send a note. That's all it takes.

Yvonne: One of our friends couldn't come. She was so distraught. We had gone to school together and had grown up together. She sent a beautiful bouquet with a note and a message that she couldn't do it. I was okay with that. She acknowledged it.

Connecting with someone who has been through it

Yvonne: What you said about really needing to talk to someone who had been through it, I was the same way. Somebody told me the story; it was probably just a few days after Brian. I was in shock with Brian. I don't know if it was my sister-in-law or my brother, but they said, "Do you know Rose's (my sister-in-law) cousin so and so?" I couldn't even concentrate at the time. "Her son died," they said, "he was 19 years old." He'd had a heart attack at nineteen. "Maybe you want to try to call her," they said. I wanted to call her so badly, and connect. My brother said she has become a recluse. I thought, "Oh my God, a recluse! Is this what is going to happen to me?" She doesn't go out in public anymore. I tried to reach her. I connected with a woman from The Compassionate Friends, but before that I was searching.

Jane: You know what, though, this is all very interesting because here, right here, shows the need. That need to connect. I still go through this. I remember when I heard about Michael. I know where I was, standing right on the stairway. Ray said, "You know Anne Dionne", and I said, "Yes." He said, "You're not going to believe what happened," and he told me. I said, "Oh, no!" I went to call Anne but her number was unlisted, so I couldn't get through. I called the pastor of our church and I said, "Her number is unlisted but I want her to know that I am here if she needs to talk to me." I go through the thing where I don't know where these people are. I identify with what I was like. You don't know, does this person want to be bothered? Does this person not? Do they want you in their life? Do they not? I think with anyone I knew at all, I would just take the chance and pick up the phone and call. It doesn't hurt to just say, "Look, is there anything I can do?" Because if they know you, and I wouldn't do it to somebody I didn't know, they know that you've been there. You do know what they are going through. You are the one person that can say, "Yes, I do know what you're going through."

Jane: That's a need that we all have, to connect. Amy, my daughter, is the same way. We got to the point where we were looking for murder-related things, victim things. It was around Christmas time, and you don't want anything to happen to you around Christmas time, as you know. Life stopped. We did connect, I should say. They came down to see us, the woman who was conducting the Omega program. She came down, and she spoke with Ray and me. The twins did start out going with us. Amy stayed longer than Drew did. Then it was just Ray and I that went.

Deb: My husband and I supported each other. He seemed to know when I was having a "Peter John moment" and most of the time I seemed to recognize his valleys as well. We were loving, patient, and very kind to each other. My family helped each other so we did not feel alone. Our daughter, however, must have felt alone because even when she finally came home she had to begin her grueling grief process.

Anger

Yvonne: Anger doesn't get you anywhere. It really doesn't. In fact, it can be dangerous.

Jane: Anger can be very destructive, and it can be counterproductive, too. You see a lot, and I'm talking again on a victim bend. I notice these things now when I see people on television. A lot of these victims are still so very angry. I've been a victim, too, but they anger me because you want to say they don't do themselves or their cause any good to be that explosive and that angry. They could do so much more if they can vent that in a more productive way. Do a walk. Do a march. You know, something like that raises awareness of something. We do that every Mother's Day.

That's what one mother does in memory of her son who was murdered on Dec. 20, I think it's about eight years ago now. Mother's Day is awful. Every Mother's Day she has a walk, and that's my time with Chris. That makes Mother's Day bearable to me, because that's my time I walk for Chris, and then I spend the rest of the day with the twins. I feel like I've done something for Chris.

Yvonne: That's a hard one. It's hard to find the right thing. It's very difficult, you know, to find the right answer.

Jane: We tried a support organization which did not have a therapist or facilitator. There was just a group of people, many of whom had these unresolved crimes, venting their anger. I mean I understand that, you know. On the other hand, when we went to Omega there were unresolved crimes, too, but we had a facilitator who was able to curb the anger and not let any one person control the meeting. There was control, where at the other meeting there wasn't. We only gave it one try anyway. They were very nice to us, but even then I can remember them saying to us, "Oh, you don't even know yet, you're still in shock." And I remember thinking; "I'm going to get worse?"

Deb: People mean well but some remarks can make us angry and hurt us.

Choices in grieving

Anne: Obviously there are a lot of things that we don't have control over, but I think in some ways we do have control over the way we grieve. You can choose to stay in the anger, bitterness, become reclusive, etc. I think that's sort of a choice. Or you can choose to do productive things like help other people, live and love more fully than you ever did before, make an effort to do those things. I really believe that it's a choice.

Yvonne: Yes, I do too. I think one of the choices that I made is that I really wanted to be the best person I could be, to really give the love.

Jane: And you wanted Brian to be proud of you.

Yvonne: Absolutely. That was so important to me.

Deb: That's true for me also.

Anne: I agree because I think that being very angry and shutting yourself off from the world, that just doesn't bring honor to your son's life at all. I think that giving to other people and living life fully brings a lot of honor and dignity to his life.

Yvonne: It does. And we have to have the hope that it will get better.

You know, would I have ever thought 17 years ago that I would have five grandchildren and one on the way? I just never thought that would happen.

How great is that? I am crazy about these kids. It just has brought so much joy. It really has. I just feel like the love I have for Brian, that I've got extra here and that I could give that to other people. You know, we've been through the worst. People say, "Gee, you're so happy go lucky." If they only knew.

Doing the funeral right for our children

Yvonne: There were three priests at Brian's funeral. All I could think of in my mind is that this is for Brian, it is the last thing that I can do right here today, to do it right. I'm not going to faint, and I'm just going to keep going.

Anne: I wonder if that's a common thing because I can very much relate to that. I remember I had nothing to wear, so the night before the funeral some of my family and a friend took me to the mall. I was just in a fog, I didn't care. We just walked around the store. I remember that. But the day of the funeral I remember standing there and hugging everybody. The foremost thing in my mind was that I wanted Michael to be proud of me. That was the only thing I could think of during that funeral. I wanted to stand upright, and be in control, and have a nice service because I wanted him to be proud of his mother.

Jane: I gave a eulogy, and that's how I felt that he was going to be proud of me. So I wrote my tribute to Chris and I gave it then. I had a backup. You know my mother used to say I was the most determined person she ever knew, and I think that day I had more determination. I just knew this was the last thing I could do for him.

Deb: My husband and I wanted our son's funeral to be a true tribute, so we planned it carefully. We asked our parents what they wanted and then waited for our daughter to come home to see what she wanted. We mixed old-fashioned traditional hymns with new Christian videos. We had meaningful Bible readings. But, our minister was new to our church and did not really know Peter John so I gave his eulogy with my husband at my side. I even got laughs when I talked about the girl friends. Upon my closing, my husband gathered his shattered nerves and said a few words. When we opened up a sharing time, we began to learn about the many wonderful things that our son had done to help other people during his short life.

Yvonne: That was very gutsy of you both.

Jane: I don't know what gave me the…It was weird because we had a couple of days between the time we had been notified until his funeral. He had to go through the medical examiner and all that stuff. His body had to be flown home. So I started on my computer just writing it out. It was my way of writing it all down, what I wanted to say to him. My brother and sister were beside me and they were kind of helping me, you know, and giving me ideas. I just felt he would have been proud, and that made me feel, you know, it was the last thing I can do for him…

About the Authors

Anne Dionne

Born in Fitchburg, MA, Anne is a Registered Nurse working for a busy Family Practice in Pepperell, MA. She serves as a chat room moderator for the National website of The Compassionate Friends, an organization which offers grief support to parents, grandparents, and siblings. She has co-founded and facilitated a bereavement support group in her vicinity called, *Picking up the Pieces*. She is involved in many church activities and shares her story of loss, as well as her faith journey, with various church groups. Anne and her husband, Steven, reside in Lunenburg, MA. They are the parents of two children, Kelly and Michael.

Deborah LeBouf Kulkkula

Deborah LeBouf Kulkkula has two masters' degrees: one in Education and one in Business Administration. Deb was recognized in Who's Who Among Students in American Colleges in 1983-4. She received the Outstanding Young Women of America Award in 1984; the Point of Excellence Award by Kappa Delta Pi for her distinguished contributions in the field of education in 1995; and The Paul D. Stackpole Memorial Humanitarian Award for her work with the bereaved in 2000.

Deb served as The Compassionate Friends newsletter editor, chapter leader, and/or ex-official chapter advisor for eleven years. In

2005, she was The Compassionate Friends National Conference Speaker/Workshop/Sharing Session Chair.

By 1992, Deb established herself as a participatory learning specialist. She wrote a learning center manual for educators, which is used by many elementary schools along the East Coast.

In 1997, she founded Word Wits Writers and Speakers Bureau. Hence, Deb has spoken about grief to a wide variety of audiences.

She and her husband Peter live in rural Fitchburg, MA in the same cottage where they raised three children: Jane, Peter John and Quy Dan Ha. Tragically since this book was written, Quy died in a car accident.

Yvonne Lancaster

Born in Worcester, MA, in 1946, Yvonne is a former newspaper columnist and author of her award winning column, *From the Heart*. She is the recipient of writing awards from United Press International, Massachusetts Press Association and New England Press Association for writing excellence. She was named Woman of the Year by the Business and Professional Women of America.

She is currently a human resources consultant and resides in Leominster, MA with her husband, Neil. Together, they have five children; Brian, Elizabeth, Timothy, Evan, and Gwenythe. They have eight grandchildren.

Jane Maki

Jane was born on Christmas day in 1939. She graduated from Boston College School of Nursing in 1961 with a BS degree in nursing. She later became board certified in gerontological nursing. She worked as a registered nurse until her retirement in 1995. Most of her career was dedicated to veterans and terminally ill patients.

In November 1965 Jane married Ray Maki. Together they had

three children: Christopher was born on Dec. 19, 1966; Andrew and Amy on July 31, 1968.

Jane is president of The Christopher Maki Memorial Foundation. She also serves on the board of directors for the Garden of Peace, a memorial to victims of homicide and the Alpha Resource Center, an organization offering help and hope to survivors of homicide victims. She has been a participant in many panels and discussion groups concerning victims of violence.

Jane says her family and extended family have been her greatest joy and her greatest treasures. By telling her story, her desire is to reach others who are either victims, or friends or relatives of victims, and share her experiences with them in the hope that they may find peace.

EPILOGUE

We, the authors of *Every Step of the Way*, and the proud mothers of our deceased sons, Michael Steven, Christopher Lars, Peter John and Brian Richard, want you to know that we have come through the worst and have survived.

During the time our sons lived on earth they were loved by their families and friends. They all had great promise for a bright future that will now never be. None of us ever imagined these terrible tragedies would take our children and leave us battling for our sanity and survival. We are optimistic and believe that you too will survive and move forward to live a life that is full and happy.

We feel that it has been our faith in God and humanity that has pulled us through. We believe we will be reunited with our sons in heaven one day.

It has been important for us to be optimistic and make a positive difference in our own lives, and in the lives of people we touch along the way. We hope we have touched you.

Printed in the United States
59379LVS00002B/99